Early Praise for Po

"WARNING LABEL: Read this book advisedly, as you will be inspired, motivated, encouraged and indeed compelled to go and do likewise. It is a life changer and you will be impacted! You have been warned!"

-David Dean
Board President, National Crime Prevention Council
Counselor to Public Officials at all Levels of Government

"Policy Walking should be required reading for every Social Science, Criminal Justice and Theology major in every college, university and seminary in the country. Jack Calhoun gets it right...really right!"

-Bob Diegelman
Former Deputy Assistant Attorney General for Policy and
Management, U.S. Department of Justice

"Jack breathes life into the normally dry terrains of policy analysis and evaluation research, weaving captivating narratives that blend the voices of social entrepreneurs and the people they seek to help while lifting our sights and illuminating the path forward."

-Clifford M. Johnson
Executive Director, Institute for Youth, Education, and Families
National League of Cities

"Inspired by his father's common refrain, 'What are you going to do about it?' and Jack's own deep inner sense of compassion and justice, Policy Walking *provides a beautifully written, fresh and compelling look at how to shape lasting community building policies.... This book tugs at your heartstrings, inspiring us all to do more.... Whether we are concerned with the culture of policing or child welfare or justice reform, Jack reminds us that, together, we will walk this path to a more just world."*

-Vikki Spruill
President and CEO, Council on Foundations

"He brings the vitality of practice, hope and a sense of compassion, offering a heartfelt corrective to the dispassionate neutrality of scholarly prose on 'what works' or is 'promising' to help youth in adverse circumstances find their way safely and productively into adulthood."

-Joan Serra Hoffman
Founding Co-Director
Inter-American Coalition for the Prevention of Violence

"Human stories of violence prevention game changers in this book inspire and give hope. America leads the world in knowledge on what prevents violence, but not on harnessing it. Get your legislator and fellow voters to start reading this book."

-Irvin Waller
Professor and Author of *Smarter Crime Control: A Guide to Safer Futures for Citizens, Communities and Politicians*
Former Secretary General International Centre
for the Prevention of Crime

"He doesn't shy away from the grim statistics or the grit of the work, and, at the same time, he lifts up the people and policies that make change possible. The author takes us through the inspiring actions of others – policy walkers – to reflect not only what is going on in communities across the country but also what change is possible."

-Rachel A. Davis
Managing Director, Prevention Institute

"As Commissioner of the Massachusetts Department of Youth Services in the mid-1970s, Jack was at the forefront of a revolution in the treatment of juvenile offenders. Skillfully navigating volatile terrain, Jack proved to the nation that a state's most troubled youth could be treated in a wide variety of rigorous, highly accountable community-based programs with only minimal reliance on secure settings."

-Michael J. Widmer
Former Deputy Chief of Staff to
Massachusetts Governor Michael Dukakis

"Jack acknowledges the difficult work we do, the obstacles we face, the lives that are lost, but, at the same time, he connects us, telling us how to lead to get the work done. He gives us hope that, even against adversity, together we can make a difference."

-Ernesto Olivares
Director, California Cities Violence Prevention Network
Former Mayor, Santa Rosa, CA

"Your passion, personal story, and professional experiences are influencing a generation."

-Tracy M. Colunga
Director, National Forum on Youth Violence Prevention
Long Beach, CA Site

POLICY WALKING

Lighting Paths to Safer Communities, Stronger Families & Thriving Youth

by John A. Calhoun

POLICY WALKING

Published by

Policy Walking:
Lighting Paths to Safer Communities,
Stronger Families & Thriving Youth

ISBN: 978-0-9972922-4-4

©2016 by John A. Calhoun
All rights reserved.

www.HopeMatters.org
www.BrandSpoken.com

Dedication

To the hundreds of heroes with whom I have linked arms,
people who have kept me, and who continue to keep me,
on my path.

Other Books by John A. Calhoun

Hope Matters: The Untold Story of How Faith Works in America

Through the Hourglass: Poems of Life and Love

CONTENTS

POLICY WALKING

Lighting Paths to Safer Communities,
Stronger Families & Thriving Youth

Do We Know What Sets Us On Our Path?

We all come to this path—this road to change, to care, to building community—with a unique gait, an individual set of circumstances, convictions, character attributes that lead us to our critical work. We push ahead at every level, working to make things better, and ultimately through this work, informing, creating, enacting policies along our paths. We are, in effect, policy walking.

But what brings us to our paths? To the street corners, to the shelters, to the youth groups, committee meetings, Congressional hearings, pulpits and podiums? I have run non-profit organizations large and small; I have served as a gubernatorial and presidential appointee; and I began my career deeply involved in youth work and community development. What brought me to my path? To some degree, it is a mystery I'll never fully unravel: some has to do with values inculcated early on, values I didn't even know I was absorbing: my mother's humor, charm and unrelenting community work, bringing to our raucous dining room table strangers, stranded college students, lonely widows (we never knew who); my father's clarity, insistence on doing a job well and on that complaints without suggestions about how you were going to address them were completely unacceptable.

For both, service was not preached; it was done naturally, without fanfare. It was an organic part of who my father and mother were. Ethel Green Newman, our nanny, played a seminal role in our lives:

her enveloping and always-ready embrace convinced us on the most fundamental of levels that, no matter how badly we had messed up, in her and God's eyes, we were wonderful, precious, unique. Some could be attributed to seismic events such as the Civil Rights Movement, some to faith, some to the "accidents" of life, as Aristotle would put it—those I met along the way, books read, life-threatening sickness encountered, eye-opening trips.

It becomes even more difficult to parse when one tries to figure out how what's in you responds to external events. One can meet a person, even an extraordinary person and nothing clicks. Yet one can meet another, as I did in a remote Native American village in Eagle, Alaska, who, it seemed, struck a deeply resonant, unarticulated chord in me, thus changing my life course dramatically, a course deepened and affirmed when I sat in Ringe High School's front row in Cambridge, Massachusetts, transfixed by a young, passionate preacher named Martin Luther King Jr. who was putting his life on the line, King inviting us to get our feet moving, to join him on his path.

I've tried to understand as best as I'm able what put me on my road. What matters most to me, however, is not why I'm on this path, but that I'm on it. And, for that, I'm profoundly grateful that I'm on it, still on it, and deeply grateful to the many who nudged, spurred, supported and inspired me along the way, and who, in many, many ways, continue to do so.

The Pressures of Pedigree

My father was born in Charleston. To find work, my grandfather journeyed to Birmingham, Alabama, to Shreveport, Louisiana, and then back. They had the name, Calhoun, and the pedigree, but, because of the Civil War, almost no money. Calhoun this, Calhoun that – streets, statues, books in windows – honoring my great-great-great uncle John C. Calhoun – a passionate second-generation leader of our young country, he served as Secretary of State, Secretary of War, and, twice, Vice President. A brilliant nationalist—at first—he

2

argued for policies and programs that "would help bind the nation." He helped spur the building of canals, roads and railroads. Then his southern roots tackled him. Guised in the cloak of "states' rights," he became an apologist for white slave owners and an advocate of secession.

For my grandmother, the "war of northern aggression" ended yesterday. Portraits of ancestors were not portraits, but shadows of obligation. My father paid. He excelled academically, became a doctor, but, unbeknownst to me until well after he died, I learned that he stuttered. Perhaps that's why he chose to become a researcher—less personal contact. That is until he met my mother, a person who could loosen anyone's tongue, make anyone feel special, and, well, wonderful.

After earning his degree, a job as doctor to the Charleston gentry awaited him. He demurred. Not only had he married a Yankee from Boston but also someone from a long line of transcendentalists and abolitionists, and, even more repellant, a Unitarian, someone who, it seemed to my grandmother, worshipped sunsets, driftwood, flowers. To my grandmother, it must have seemed that her only son was sleeping with the enemy—the enemy, the conqueror, a heathen and someone who "cooked north." My father was supposed to reclaim the name and status. He didn't. He struck out on his own. I never understood why. I think I do now.

As he had no money growing up, my father needed financial help, which was provided by a benefactress, a Charleston aristocrat. When she died, eight "names" had to serve on her funeral pall—a Lownes, Turhune, Parker, Ravenell (cannot believe I remember), three others, and a Calhoun. My dad couldn't, or wouldn't, attend. At 14, I was sent to the funeral as his surrogate.

This is what I remember. I entered one of the lovely houses facing the Battery, the beautiful Charleston Harbor. As I looked like the flower delivery boy, no one paid much attention to me—that is, until I mentioned my name. Then the waters parted. The red carpet unrolled.   Fun and flattering, but, after a while, scary.   Their acknowledgement of me had nothing to do with me. I could have been a doddering, drooling idiot, but, in front of a Calhoun, one genuflected. I had no idea that my name meant anything. I could have been Jones.

Who knew what hopes and dreams lay beneath the name for my father? We grew up north of the Mason-Dixon line. I don't think he stayed north for ideological reasons. I think it was more for psychic survival. What courage it must have taken to refuse the siren song of a good job, status, and the iron pull of his mother. He said no, and for that I admire him.

How might his example have influenced my choice of paths? It may have been less the *choice* of a path and more an attribute, a character trait, in this case *courage* to stay on a path, courage in the face of extreme pressure. Knowing he would endorse whatever path I chose, he taught me, without saying it, the importance of purpose over pedigree.

Paternal Roots in Policy

He became a doctor for a company that made products drawn from steaming chemical baths. He supervised clinics in more than half-a-dozen sites in the mid-Atlantic region, discovering high incidences of lung-related diseases. A researcher at heart, he kept numbers. And the numbers alarmed him. Workers were getting seriously ill. Subsequently, he made changes in ventilation, increased monitoring air quality and exposure, and elevated the caliber of the clinics in all the plants. Owners were not happy with the expense, but they reluctantly followed through on his recommendations and respiratory complaints dropped dramatically. When he died, he was cited as a "pioneer in industrial medicine," then a nascent field. This would probably fall under the aegis of public health and worker safety today. In this, he may have taught me policy change lessons: patience, persistence, the need to persuade those over whom he had little or no power, and the importance of an ultimate goal.

Paternal and Maternal Gifts

My father needed clear and predictable structure to shore up his internal insecurity. When all was in place at home, he was charming, engaging and witty. When it wasn't, often true in a house with four kids and many guests, watch out. He could get angry quickly. Thus the predictable pieces had to be re-established quickly. My mother, deeply secure, could form a community in a tornado.

I would describe him as a moderate, civic-minded Republican. If something was wrong, he refused to hear complaints or levy blame. His most common refrain: "What are you going to do about it?" This was not mere rhetoric. He modeled these words, serving at different times as chair of both the school and library boards.

He enjoyed speaking with guests, usually focusing on the externals such as health, school, what books were being read, etc. My sisters' many suitors had to have a great deal of confidence when sitting down for a conversation with—or grilling by—Doctor Calhoun.

My mother tended to focus on the internal: what people were thinking, what made them happy, what challenges they faced, but, above all, an uncanny ability to connect, to find deep resonance with another. It was amazing to watch: people would ask my mother a question, and, within a few minutes, there would be a mid-air flip, and her interlocutor would be sharing not simply what they did, but who they were. She developed trust faster than anyone I knew. Also, before the unwary knew it, they were helping with dishes, painting the kitchen, weeding the garden. Even after the inevitable breakups, my sisters' ex-boyfriends would return just to be part of the family happenings. We never quite knew who would be around the dinner table. She was also funny. Very funny. Once, toward the end of her life, she, in a wheelchair, went through the security screen at the airport, which beeped loudly. To the TSA agent she said, "Will you search me? That will be fun." She was also a wily strategist. As a member of her retirement community, she discovered that a large and distressing number of residents were having a hard time—even getting into accidents—when turning onto the main road from the community grounds. She tracked down a person at Pennsylvania's Department of Transportation who, it seemed, was the ultimate traffic light decider. "How do you determine where to put up traffic lights?" she asked. "We count. We stretch a black counter across the road, measure the activity and then decide." They got the black strip. My mother then told all the residents to shop more inefficiently than they had ever shopped: make one trip for eggs, return and go out again for cheese and again for milk. The nursing home got its traffic light.

For my mother, her table was your table. Her beliefs came to us not through ideology, but through what she did. She lived what she believed. She was quick to bring food to a sick neighbor. After graduating from Radcliffe in the 1929, she journeyed from Cambridge, Massachusetts, to Spellman College in Atlanta (all black) to volunteer and to help teach. This during the height of the Jim Crow laws.

She was also a risk taker—in her everyday life and in her heart of hearts. My father was not. For him, all had to be certain, predictable and safe (he absolutely hated to travel and was always a mess when en route). While my father did push intellectual boundaries, all else had to be certain, predictable. Not so my mother. "Try this…try that…you never know what you will discover…." I knew in my bones of her full support when I took a different route, such as entering seminary on short notice, joining the Civil Rights Movement, spurning ordination to teach and then to work in the inner city, as a youth worker and community organizer.

She, too, immersed herself deeply in community activities: she worked with the Polio Parent's Club, often gift-wrapping packages well into the night; she helped run Girl and Cub Scouts and, it seemed, was always involved in a political campaign, our dining room table festooned with stacks of campaign flyers. And whom she lassoed for dinner was a constant surprise. Her community work didn't reflect dour obligation. Quite the reverse. She reveled in it. She didn't talk about her work. She modeled it, as did my father. Service was not appended to your life; rather, it was an integral part of it. It was how you led your life.

And for both, you kept your word. If you didn't, severe punishment ensued. If you said you'd do something, woe to you if you went back on your word. Violating your word assumed high crime status. If you pledged to get something done, you did it, no matter how many nights and weekends it took. We were viewed as responsible people (at least potentially), people obliged to keep their word and fulfill commitments to others.

If I did worry—unfairly punished, the injustice of life, the impossibility of three sisters—I often wound up sitting on Ethel Green Newman's knee, Ethel, an African American from Georgia. She would tell me how wonderful I was, how God loved all his children, especially me (even though I was a frequent offender). She would sing. She would laugh, and she'd usually give me a piece of deep-fried, crispy chicken or a fresh biscuit with gravy. She, a woman of the deepest and most natural faith I had seen and felt up to that point in my life. Nanny, yes, but an integral part of our family. We attended the local Episcopal church with its comforting (and predictable) liturgy and rich hymns, but it was Ethel who sowed the seeds of real faith. She spoke ill of no one. Quite the reverse: bad *actions* were always an aberration. We were basically good, very good, wonderful. The smell of her amazing cooking and her laughter filled the house. She was the go-to person for all of us in times of trouble. She was family throughout our entire childhood and well into our college days.

From my parents, I absorbed commitment, service, trust in our abilities and the obligation to use these abilities. And we knew we were loved and supported. We knew that we were to honor the stranger and that we were obliged to step up whatever the situation. This wasn't really told: it was expected. And when we messed up, or when things really got clanky in the family, we wound up in Ethel's unquestioning, affirming embrace.

In Pain and Near Death

In second grade, I contracted polio, one of the most virulent strains, bulbar, which attacked and rendered my lungs almost completely useless. I don't know how this played a part in my eventual choice of paths, but I'm certain, on some level, that it did. I was out of circulation for almost a year. I recall the pain, the fear, the loneliness: the hours in the "iron lung" that breathed for me, the heavy World War II woolen blankets suffused with steam, rough, prickly blankets always almost scalding, it seemed, draped over young muscles in danger of atrophy. I recall trauma-induced nightmares that stayed with me for almost a decade, nightmares with almost the same theme: a huge slag heap hovering over a village about to bury it, suffocate it. Slated for death if not permanent disability, I miraculously survived, no, thrived with no residual effects. I still wonder how this, on an unconscious level, influenced my choice of paths. Perhaps it gave me a keen sense of another's pain. Perhaps the real gift may have been unquenchable joy, absolutely undeterred hope. If I could survive that cylindrical machine that breathed for me, survive my imminent death, anything thereafter had to be a gift.

Heroes

Who fully knows the real reasons for one's chosen path or paths? But sometimes deeply embedded, often-unarticulated values rise to the visible and articulate level by accident. I spent one summer in Eagle, Alaska, working in a Native American community, spurred both by adventure and a need for space—lots of it—space to get away from a serious relationship that wasn't working. In Eagle, I met Episcopal "missioners," the Reverend Murray Trelease and Bishop Gordon, both former Air Force pilots whose muscular and organic faith stunned me. Each could move easily from conducting Holy Communion (Mass) to helping repair a house, deliver food, or sit for hours with the lonely.

8

Their work seemed natural, full and sustaining. I wanted part of it. I changed my plans suddenly, enrolling first in the Church Divinity School of the Pacific in Berkeley, California, and the following year transferring to the Episcopal Divinity School in Cambridge, Massachusetts. By the end of my second year (of three), I decided, in part because of the burgeoning Civil Rights Movement, to reject ordination and life as a parish priest, choosing instead work in the civil rights and community/youth-development arenas. It was a secular path to be sure, one laid by my parents, by people of deep commitment to social change and by people of faith, people who hardly spoke of their faith, but lived it.

I continue to meet heroes along my path: the woman who lost two children to gang violence who now has "400 neighborhood children"; the 10-year-old in the Chicago housing projects singing to the elderly as her service project; a street worker standing between an assailant with a gun and a potential victim. And so many more, people who both inspire and sustain, people who keep me on my path.

Thus, my choice of heroes should come as no surprise. Other than my parents, if I had to pick three, they would be these three. Dr. Martin Luther King Jr., whose message of social justice was not only preached but lived, his a willingness to put himself at the mercy of unjust laws, his a hard path I can only imagine. Dr. King derailed whatever college teaching aspirations I may have harbored. Second, Andy Gayak, an old, gruff Hungarian prospector living in Eagle, Alaska, whom I met while doing youth work with the Native American community living there. Virulent segregation existed: the "Indians" lived three miles away from the white community. Andy, who had no time for or interest in the church, was the only white who allowed the villagers into his truck. He saved them the three-mile trek to town, picking them up to shop, to go to the movies (8mm shown on a sheet in the general store), keep a doctor's appointment and buy supplies. And he just did it: no talking about it, no self-righteousness. He taught me how to pan gold in freezing streams. I failed, gleaning only a few flecks. Just before leaving Eagle, he reached under his bed, pulled out a small jar, fished through it, and pulled out a nugget, the largest one. He gave it to me. I was stunned. How to honor him and his memory? I had the nugget melted and fashioned into wedding rings my wife and I have worn for 44 years. And Father Paul Washington, head pastor, Church of the Advocate, in north Philadelphia, at the time, the roughest, most gang-infested section of the city. For two summers, I served as his seminarian, running youth groups, administering his summer camp, and, because the Civil Rights Movement was then in full swing, attending meetings of SNCC (Student Nonviolent Coordinating Committee), CORE (Congress of Racial Equality) or picketing the then-segregated Girard College. Father Paul was the gentlest man I have ever met. While he would attend (or host) most of these meetings in the evening, he would, during the day, feed the hungry, counsel the lost, attend to his pastoral duties. My enduring memory: the well-known, local prostitute stumbled into a particularly contentious civil rights meeting one night. Father Paul went over to her immediately. I'll never forget his eyes: amidst the din, he looked at her as if she were the only and the most beloved person in the world. Never in my life had I seen in a single person the combination of keen, strategic "horizontal" skills (program and policy, in this case work in the civil rights arena) with the "vertical" —the ability to touch and acknowledge the essential personhood of another.

And so…

For me, on the deepest and probably unarticulated level, I knew that I was precious, a child of a loving God, a God who would dust me off after a screw up, telling me to get back on the field, to quit worrying about myself, to get back to helping, to loving: as I was acknowledged by love, so was I commissioned to show that love to others.

And so my walk began…

Why I Wrote this Book

"Keep your hand on the plow, hold on."
- as sung by Mahalia Jackson, American gospel singer

In the pages that follow, I want to share with you information about violence prevention, community well-being, and youth development programs and policies that work. You can get more exhaustive descriptions from various websites or academic journals, but here, I've tried to do something different. I want to show you that policies are more than paper and politics, that, at their heart, policies are of people—made by people, to help people. That policies come alive and work when people pick them up and walk with them. I want to inspire you—to reach you wherever you are on your walk with policy, whether in the field running programs, or designing them on the local, county, state, and federal levels. I want you to look up from this book saying, "Yes, I can do that! I should do that!"

And, for those who are tired, I hope these profiles re-ignite that spark that got you started in the first place, remind you why you embarked on your particular path—your policy walk.

You have your hands "on the plow." But what stars, what vision keeps your hand on the plow, keeps you plowing? By describing the programs and policies through the eyes of those who run them—who walk them—and those who have benefitted from them, and the values and principles that keep their feet under them, my goal is to provide you with both inspiration and information.

Janet Finch embodies both the core purpose of my book, and how it is constructed. Janet served as my keynote speaker when I was sworn in as the United States Commissioner of the Administration for Children, Youth and Families (ACYF). As Commissioner, I would oversee such programs as Head Start, Child Welfare, The Center to Prevent Child Abuse and Neglect, the Office of Domestic Violence, and the Office for Families. On the occasion of my swearing-in, Janet wore what she could afford—a cheap polyester suit. Half her teeth were missing, but the courage, tenacity, and accomplishments of this woman had inspired me. I wanted her to inspire others, remind them of the very heartbeat of the agency I was about to run.

I did not want those who attended my swearing-in to hear about what I'd done in Massachusetts as Commissioner of the Department of Youth Services (DYS) —what programs I'd run, what policies I'd helped to institute or change. No, I wanted people to hear from someone who had benefitted from our policies, someone who had helped to change them; I wanted policy to live, breathe, and walk on that day. I wanted people to see and feel policy. Janet did walk it, she talked it, and, oh, how she inspired. There were few dry eyes in the crowd as Janet told her story.

At some point during my tenure as DYS Commissioner, I realized that well over 60 percent of those committed by the courts to DYS had been in multiple foster care placements, some as many as seven. In the process, these young people felt ever more unworthy ("trash" as one young man described it) and ever more removed from their families, neighborhoods, and local schools. At the time, services from child welfare, mental health, and DYS staff focused almost exclusively on the child, a legitimate principle on the face of it: children might have to be removed from terribly abusive or neglectful or trauma-inducing environments, and sometimes fast. But few, if any, of the offered services attempted to strengthen families, to find whatever positive shreds of family might exist and build on those.

With help from a private foundation, we created a pilot program for a small group of mothers of delinquent youth. The program's design was profoundly simple. Mothers would meet in each other's homes once a week. A psychiatrist (Yitzak Bikal, the only psychiatrist I could find willing to leave his office) met with the mothers in their homes, usually sitting in a circle with them. The mothers, most of them dysfunctional, had to clean up their homes and prepare food. They set goals for each other, much like Weight Watchers or AA. They swapped phone numbers, agreeing to support each other during the week. Janet had seven children. The Department of Child Welfare had four of them; my agency, DYS, had three. An angry woman, Janet demanded that the state that had "captured" her children, return them. "No," said Dr. Bakal, "you have to show that you can be a good mother; get off drugs, and get a job or go back to school."

Janet told her story the day of my swearing-in, beginning with, "My children had been seen by school adjustment counselors, mental health workers, probation, and now the Department of Youth Services. But nobody talked to me. Nobody tried to help me be a better mother. You see, no mother wants to lose her kids. And, when you start losing them, you take something or drink something to take your pain away. I failed as a mother. I couldn't live with my failure, so I got as high as I could to fly away from my pain." Over a period of two years, Janet began to stabilize. No, more than that, Janet began to claim her future. As she put it, "The state gave me back my kids. Slowly. One by one. I am a mother again."

In 1980, at the very end of the Carter administration, and in the waning days of my tenure as Commissioner of ACYF, Congress passed PL96-272, the landmark Child Welfare and Adoption Act of 1980. In cooperation with the Children's Defense Fund and other child advocates, we at ACYF designed the bill and leaned heavily on

Congress to pass it. The bill fundamentally changed child welfare practice. If a family was deemed unfit to raise children, and if a child had to be removed, a "permanency" plan had to be developed. Family strengths had to be assessed and if found, improved—"strengths" viewed widely, including father, mother, aunt, uncle, or grandparents. If family-focused services proved ineffective, all services would then focus on adoption. Thus, foster care would become a way station to permanency rather than a dumping ground—permanency, meaning either return home to a strengthened or strengthening family, or to adoption.

Dr. Wade Horn, a former ACYF Commissioner, one of my successors, called the Child Welfare and Adoption Act "one of the three most important laws affecting children in the last 100 years." The very heartbeat of this seminal law? Janet Finch.

In this book, I describe programs that work and reflect on the principles and values that have sustained me over the years as well as values that have sustained others. I know these programs well, for I have helped to create some of them, or I know the directors well, or I have personally seen the program in action. In addition, I share with you the seven key lessons I've learned along the way, lessons that include externals that influence what we do and my views on leadership (some of them hard-won). I want you to know about hopeful programs, but, more importantly, I want you to know about those who run them, and those who are served by them. Programs celebrated in this book range from the earliest intervention, "Nurse-Family Partnership," through programs designed to reclaim crime-ridden neighborhoods, to programs that mobilize entire cities, and still other programs that embrace and restore those on the far end of the spectrum, namely those returning from long stays in prison.

Let me point out what's NOT here. Were I to write about promising programs for vulnerable children, their families and the fragile communities in which they live, programs such as Head Start, Achievement Mentoring, Olweus Bullying Prevention, Functional

Family therapy, trauma-based care run by health departments, to name only a few, my book would hit the 1,000-page plus mark. Much is already available about these vital programs. I encourage you to seek them out.

In addition, I've not described in detail two well-known and promising interventions—mentoring and afterschool programs. These programs exist in schools throughout America and are a staple for the nation's large youth-serving organizations—the YM and YWCA, Big Brother Big Sisters of America (BBBS) and the Boys & Girls Clubs of America. Frankly, it proved difficult for me to select one from the many programs they run. However, many of the programs and approaches described in this book rest on principles shared by these three wonderful agencies. And, to some degree, I know of their pioneering work: I contracted with the Boys and Girls Club in Massachusetts to work with some of the state's most difficult young offenders. I know of BBBSA's commitment in Philadelphia to find mentors for troubled youth few are willing to mentor, and I know of the Y's commitment to troubled street youth in Chicago. What they have to offer should be explored by those who work with our nation's youth.

There are, however, two remarkable and related highly successful programs that are so unique that they defy categorization. Chicago's Becoming a Man and Working on Womanhood combine school-based cognitive therapy groups with mentoring, service projects and exposure to the city's cultural life. They are the subject of Chapter 3.

Finally, I have referenced, but not described, restorative justice, which involves and engages local people and victims in resolving problems. RJ, as it is known, is a highly promising and frequently used intervention that can be used as an alternative to courts. I simply have not been as close to it as I was many years ago in Massachusetts when I launched Justice as Reconciliation (formally labeled "Urban Court"). RJ is a critically important crime prevention, community-binding tool.

It is a gift to do this work, and we all take different paths to it. While each of our paths is unique, this we share: the principles, the values, the desire to change the life trajectories of those facing bleak futures, those living in chaotic families and mistrusting communities.

I want your mind to appreciate the policy and your feet to start moving … or to keep moving. And I want you to know that you are not alone.

I also want you to know this: you've got to stay close to the ground no matter how exalted your position, and you've got to stay equally close to a vision so you'll get through the inevitable snags, rocky places, and mire. Mahalia Jackson with power and poignancy urges us to "Keep your hand on the plow," knowing there is a prize beyond the blisters. We know you cannot plow straight unless you have your eye on a star. You're going to get tired. You are going to get blisters.

It takes the plow and your sustaining vision—your stars.

If I've done nothing else with my book, I want you to feel a surge— or a re-surge—of optimism. Pete Seeger, the renowned folk singer and social justice advocate, remained determinedly optimistic throughout his life. "The key to the future of the world," he said, "is finding the optimistic stories and letting them be known."

I have made every effort to do the same here. I owe the people you will meet here a profound debt of gratitude for their stories of struggle and success, for the lives they have changed and the policies they have helped to generate. They have inspired me, and, at every turn in my path, they have quickened my step.

And may they do the same for yours.

CHAPTER 1

"Hey, Loved One"

"If you look deeply into their eyes, you won't see the tattoos."

- Steve Velasquez, Peacekeeper

POLICY

We need all the good programs we've created for youth on the edge—
mentoring, afterschool programs, remedial education, job training,
and more—but with all of our programs, are we bringing them to these
youth in the best way? Do we start with labels, "trouble, delinquent,
dyslexic, abused," or do we begin with "Hey, loved one," and then,
only then, deal with the wound? We are good, so very skilled at
diagnosing and affirming the malady; but are we good at affirming the
essential humanity, the person? For this our tools are blunter. The
real work, the effective work starts by establishing loving, trusting
relationships, and succeeds through a commitment to work with and
stay with troubled youth, and to work in and stay in the most violent
communities. No one walks that policy like Kevin Grant.

WALKING

I spoke with Kevin Grant by phone from DC in late September 2015,
he sitting in a parking lot at Fairmont Hospital in Oakland, California,
waiting for the family of a gunshot victim to arrive, a family hell-bent
on revenge. "They call it doing town business," he said. "Using the

business end of the pistol is what it means. It's not the cycle of life for these kids," he continued over his scratchy cell phone, "it's the cycle of death. Second, third, even fourth generation of poverty, dads in jail, drugs, guns, no future. I'm out here with my team trying to break that cycle."

I had met Kevin about ten years earlier, having heard about his remarkable work as a street worker, his magic with tough kids, his fearlessness, effectiveness and humor. I didn't just want to talk to Kevin; I wanted to see and feel what he did. So I found myself in a car about midnight in West Oakland with Kevin, Billy Dupes, and Jay Jimenez, all three ex-cons who had turned their lives around. It didn't take long for the trash talking to start. Billy asked me what kind of car I had. I told him. He said, "Man, you'll never make it with that. You gotta get a low rider." Then my clothes, shirt and tie, totally inappropriate for where we were. "Man," continued Billy, "if you're going to do this work, you gotta get new threads."

My turn: "Okay, it's 11:30 at night. You see a group of guys on the corner, probably gang members. You get out of the car. If you're so good, what are your first words, what do you say?" Without a second's hesitation, Jay said, "Hey, loved one." "What?" I said, astounded. "Or maybe," Jay continued, "hey, nephew." I was stunned. But it soon dawned on me: a fellow gang member is a "homeboy" or "homie." "Home." the language of family. "Loved one… Nephew…" strikes a similar chord in these youth, a chord rarely played by others. Kevin, with his team, helps to administer two initiatives, "Call-ins" and "Cure Violence," both cited as "best practices," namely programs that have proven to work. Cure Violence began in Chicago, Call-Ins in Boston.

Cure Violence, founded by public health epidemiologist Dr. Gary Slutkin, takes a medical approach to a social problem and "stops the spread of violence in communities by using the methods and strategies associated with disease control—detecting and interrupting conflicts, identifying and treating the highest risk individuals, and changing social norms." It has been proven to reduce shootings and retaliatory murders. Cure Violence trains community outreach workers, such as Kevin and his team, to detect and interrupt violence, alter the behavior of at-risk individuals and teach community members better ways to solve disputes.

Spurred by escalating rates of violent crime, Operation Ceasefire began in Boston in the mid-1990s. Planners understood that only a few highly active offenders were responsible for a majority of the city's serious crime problem. Project creator David Kennedy and colleagues "from enforcement, city officials, the community and street outreach workers designed the Call-in, a face-to-face meeting with gang members in a forum setting." (Wikipedia). The Call-in, a highly structured meeting, is similar to a scripted drama in which law enforcement, the service community, community members and offenders with long records participate. Top law enforcement officials lead, conveying the message that violence must stop, must stop now and that if any further offenses occur, any, that the offender will serve time, a great deal of time. Law enforcement also conveys the message that they don't want to send people away, that the offenders have a choice. The service community then offers choices, such as drug abuse counseling, job training, mentoring, housing, etc. Finally, a community member speaks, "the moral voice of the community," usually someone who has lost a relative to violence. Kennedy puts it succinctly: "We're here to help you. If you don't let us help you, we are here to stop you." Highly-trained street workers, sometimes called "peacekeepers" or "violence interrupters," many or most of whom have records themselves, help the offenders follow through on their commitments after the Call-in. The immediate result of Operation Ceasefire was a 63 percent reduction in youth homicide and a 30 percent reduction in homicide citywide, what has been called the Boston Miracle.

These describe the programs' basic elements, each underscoring the essential role played by workers on the street. However, no formal program description can convey the passion, commitment, courage, and hope needed to do this life-and-death work successfully.

Kevin, who won the California Peace Prize in 2012, does. He both embodies the work and transcends its description.

Kevin served time, plenty of it—25 years. He returned from jail, and, in 1992 started working with parolees, helping them to get jobs, drug treatment, "whatever was needed." He found he was good at it: those on the street needing his help trusted him, and he forged equally trusting relationships with those in city and county agencies—schools, law enforcement, probation and public health to name a few. He convinced local businesses, Target, Safeway, and others, to hire ex-offenders. "But life kept getting in the way. Violence at home. Violence on the street. Petty beefs that wind up with somebody dead. They don't have nobody to talk to, nobody they trust. We're that trust."

His job development work morphed into a "Street Outreach" program, which he helped to design. "We do a slow dance with these 'loved ones.'" Loved ones? "You see, it's got to start with a relationship, with trust, and then the job stuff, counseling, that all comes next. They're not gonna go to counseling or job training 'cause it's there. They go because we say it's okay. We 'tag them in.'" "Tag-in" is a street term for induction into a gang—"induction," a tepid description of a usually violent process. With Kevin, the term means approval, giving the okay to something, usually joining or signing up for something like a job or counseling. They need Kevin's endorsement. He continues: "They go because it will be a big change for them, and they're scared. And they need support and they're too proud and scared and tough to admit they're scared. We're conduits of trust. People have given up on them. They're veterans of every service out there. Why didn't these services take?" Kevin asks. "'Cause nobody walked with them, and stayed with them at night when they were scared or drunk or couldn't figure out how to read the text or fill out a driver's license application."

Street Outreach has evolved into a highly structured initiative. Kevin has a three-tiered team. Training is constant. In addition to the more formal trainings, Kevin checks in weekly with staff, which allows workers to vent, to "get their needle back up from empty 'cause one of their best kids might have been shot and killed."

But under the structure, or, more accurately, suffusing all of it, is the commitment to building relationships, to building trust. "If we ain't real, nothing's going to happen." "What's real?" I ask. He replies, "Not giving up. Being there at the right time—their time, not our time. And they ain't clients. They're 'loved ones.' See they've been clients most of their young lives, but nobody's been real to them."

"I'll tell you the difference between a client and a 'loved one.' We got one kid a job, a pretty good job. But it was early, man, real early. Me or one of my guys picked him up at 4:00 in the morning so he could start work at 5:00. And he made it. If you ain't got love, you ain't gonna get yourself out the bed in the dark, especially if you've been on the streets the night before trying to stop the shooting. And there was another kid, always in trouble, but he loved that PlayStation, would play it for hours. So I bought him one, and he stayed at home playing it. Wasn't out with his boys. People asked me why I took money out my pocket for him. Well, I told them, I asked 'What would my son want?' PlayStation made it. Made it big time. Got a job. Got a family, and a house. He sometimes helps me with my kids, coming in to speak with them, telling them he was in their shoes, that he knows what they're going through, who they are, and that they can make it."

It's what Kevin actually sees under the tangle of anger, fear and hopelessness in the youth with whom he works. Kevin's moving description of the difference between "client" and "loved one," evoked two powerful memories. The first was from a conversation I had with Steve Velasquez, a "Peacekeeper" from Santa Rosa, California, engaged in the same tough work as Kevin in Oakland. Although our conversation occurred many years ago, it stuck. When discussing how to get to the heart of mistrusting youth, Steve said simply, "If you look deeply into their eyes, you won't see the tattoos."

Kevin's stirring testimony brought me back to a book I hadn't read since my days in seminary, Martin Buber's *I and Thou*. Buber claims that most of us live in an "I-It" world, a world to be used or controlled as opposed to a world to be met. Real listening, maintains Buber, is not waiting for the other person to take a breath, but to fully be. "The inborn Thou is realized in the lived relations with that which meets it" (Buber, Martin, *I and Thou*, Charles Scribner's Sons, 1958, p. 27). Such deep listening is not without risk. Those seeking the essential Thou, as Kevin, cannot hold back, for getting to Thou "can only be spoken with the whole being" (p.10).

Kevin lives Buber's theology. As Kevin seeks to find and nurture the essential "thou" in others he, in turn, finds his essential "I." In Buber's terms: "I become through my relationship to the Thou; as I become I, I say Thou" (ibid., p. 11).

It also brought to me an old Hasidic tale someone sent me after a speech I gave, a speech in which I referenced Kevin's search for his "loved ones." The rabbi asks his students, "How can we determine the hour of dawn, when the night ends and the day begins?" One of his students suggested, "When from a distance you can distinguish between a dog and a sheep?" "No," came the answer from the rabbi. "Is it when one can distinguish between a fig tree and a grapevine?" ventured a second student. "No," replied the rabbi. "Please tell us the answer, then," pleaded the students. "It is," said the wise teacher, "when you can look into the face of human beings and you have enough light in you to recognize them as your brothers and sisters. Up until then, it is night, and darkness is still with us."

One cannot go for more than a minute while speaking with Kevin without hearing at least one of these— "my son... loved ones... blessings..." He and his team subscribe to both the Call-In and Violence Interruption models. According to Kevin, both models rest on two fundamental tenets that are hardly prominent in the descriptions: establishing loving, trusting relationships, and a commitment to work in and stay in the most violent communities. "We are known not just as helpers, but as people. We go to their barbeques, to their community meetings and to school events. Yeah, we're there when the shooting begins; we're there to comfort the families and to stop retaliation, and we're there when nothing's happening." He breaks his team into three parts: the outreach team that connects with and develops community resources, those that are in the community, attending events and church suppers, keeping their ears to the ground, and the violence interrupters, "the hot team."

Kevin has witnessed it all: bullet-ridden bodies; mothers with their son's brain parts spattered over them. "I'm here to take the pain. One change we made in the program: get to the hospital fast. Even beat the family there. Decisions are made when a loved one comes out his coma, even with all kinds of tubes sticking outta him. I want mine to be the first face he sees. The first. Then I got to calm the family down, too. They got grief, but they're ready to do business, too. They love their boy. Then we're gonna be together to put him on the right path and keep him there. And you gotta be ready to do anything – help clear a rap sheet, getting gift cards for clothes, 'cause when you're shot and in the hospital, they rip all your clothes off, shoes too, looking for other bullet holes. Anything. You wouldn't believe it: I helped put in a toilet riser so the family has a toilet with water in it. And you've got to stand out in the rain, too," he adds. "We don't close at 5:00."

Kevin feels things have changed since he began—less community and family support, fewer jobs, an overreaction to even the smallest slight and "guns everywhere." "Man," he says, "we're fighting this thing with a water pistol."

What would he change if he had the power? More loving support, getting guns off the street, and effective job training programs. "You see, these kids tell me they can make it on fifteen to twenty dollars an hour. But see, they go to these training programs, and at the end of them there either ain't no jobs or they can have one for seven dollars an hour."

I asked Kevin how he looked at his life, and what he could point to as a result of his work. "Well, I found my focus." "Your calling," I put in. "No," he replied, "that's too strong. I didn't get zapped by Him, and I think I'm on His hit list anyway. Let's just say 'my focus.' People know I'm righteous, too." For Kevin, that word holds no theological connotation at all. It means being honorable, reliable, trustworthy, a man who gives his word and keeps it. "Man, even when I screw up, drop a ball, or miss an appointment, people say, 'Kev, that's okay. We know you busy.' They know I'm righteous. I can go into hospitals, police stations and into the worst community, the worst house on the block and they'll trust me."

"I know we've saved lives. Lots of them. We've lost lives, too."

I told Kevin he was a beacon, an inspiration for so many. He was for me when I met him almost 10 years ago, when I drove around West Oakland with him at midnight, watching him work, watching him get out of the car and talking to youth gathered on the corner. He didn't want to hear it. "Jack, you see I'm really very selfish. I get more hugs from more people and more different people than anybody I know. Tell me a job that gives you that."

RESOURCES

- .• Cure Violence (Chicago-based) – (http://cureviolence.org/) From its website: "Cure Violence stops the spread of violence in communities by using the methods and strategies associated with disease control – detecting and interrupting conflicts, identifying and treating the highest risk individuals, and changing social norms."
- National Network for Safe Communities (New York-based)- (http://nnscommunities.org/) - From its website: "The National Network for Safe Communities supports cities implementing proven strategic interventions to reduce violence and improve public safety, minimize arrest and incarceration, strengthen communities, and improve relationships between law enforcement and the communities it serves. The National Network is committed to building a community of practice that operates along a set of guiding principles: First, do no harm. Strengthen communities' capacity to prevent violence. Enhance legitimacy. Offer help to those who want it. Get deterrence right. Use enforcement strategically."
- Buber, Martin, *I And Thou*, Charles Scribner's and Sons, 1958

POLICY WALKING

CHAPTER 2

Nurse-Family Partnership:
Changing Futures Two at a Time

"My life was a mess—dad in jail, no job, nobody to turn to, everything going wrong, I couldn't manage anything and here I had this baby coming. I was going to make a mess of another life."

-Nafessa with 1-year-old Noah, at a Nurse-Family Partnership (NFP) meeting, Philadelphia, PA, Nov. 11, 2015

"This job is the best nursing job I ever had. You're so busy in a hospital job, running back and forth, no time for a relationship. You're always entering data. The patients leave. They don't come back. Here we build a relationship, a two-year relationship. I have a hand in building a future, two futures! Really, they're not clients. They become part of a family. This is not a job; it's a calling."

-Joy Ahn, BSN, RN, Nurse Home Visitor, at the same meeting

POLICY

The quality of life prospects for a first time, low-income mother bearing a child out of wedlock are, if not grim, highly uncertain. The prospects portend a life of trouble, an onset or continuation of poverty, conflict and despair for each. Statistics tell the story: children born in such circumstances have a dramatically higher incidence of abuse, neglect, foster care placement, dropping out of school and juvenile justice system involvement. Sound science bears it out.

While working in an inner-city day care center, Dr. David Olds, a young professor of pediatrics, psychiatry and preventative medicine, realized that children born in compromised circumstances needed help much earlier—at home with their mother, and before birth. Olds spotted significant brain development difficulties at four years of age. He saw lessened affection, and more aggressiveness and inattention. He saw babies in high-stress environments bathed constantly in cortisol. Cortisol affects brain structures setting individuals on a fight-or-flight hair trigger pattern throughout their lives. This, an adaptation useful in prehistory, serves to damage today. Such children, so alert to uncertainty and danger, so unable to escape toxic stress, cannot concentrate, cannot learn well, cannot easily forge bonds of affection.

Olds began a nurse home visiting program, targeting first-time mothers and refining it over the years. Olds based it on the knowledge that during the first 30 months of a child's life, basic functions related to vision, hearing, language development and emotional stability are being set. He believed that, during this early window of opportunity, the experiences of trained, registered nurses could have a huge impact on both mother and child. He was right, resoundingly right. In the twenty-year follow-up to his original randomized control trials, he learned that the children who received these services were significantly less likely to wind up entangled in various government systems such as child welfare, mental health, and the criminal justice system. Olds consequently won the Stockholm Award for Crime Prevention.

WALKING

Loaded down with paper, studies, reports and a variety of program descriptions I visited the Nurse-Family Partnership offices on Delaware Avenue in North Philadelphia. One enters a light-filled, open space flanked by a kitchen (the alluring smell of chili) and tables both large, for adults and small, for kids. I met with a roomful of about 15 nurses, their supervisors and their administrator, Dr. Katherine Kinsey, "a recovering academic." We were joined by two young mothers, one with Noah in her lap. The conversation—open, honest, mutually supportive, fun and joyous conveyed a profound sense of mission. Everyone should be so fortunate just to be able to inhale the atmosphere—the supportive aura in the face of the tough work NFP nurses perform.

Nurse-Family Partnership: the Program

"She wouldn't let me go. She kept calling me. I thought she was crazy. Why would she care about me? Finally I gave up. I said yes. I was so alone. When we sat down, she listened to me. Listened to me for two hours! She gave me so much advice. I didn't feel like a client. She's not really a nurse; she's a friend."

-Samia, young mother

Formally described, NFP, based on the pioneering work of Dr. Olds, is an evidence-based, community health program that helps transform the lives of vulnerable mothers pregnant with their first child, mothers at the greatest risk of suffering significant health, education, and economic difficulties. Each vulnerable new mom is partnered with a registered nurse early in her pregnancy and receives ongoing nurse home visits. NFP helps families—and the communities they live in—become stronger while saving money for local, state and federal governments.

NFP has three goals:

- Improved pregnancy outcomes, by helping maximize parental health
- Improved child health and development by helping parents provide responsible and competent care
- Improved economic self-sufficiency of the family by helping parents plan for their future

Stunning Results

Subject to randomized control group testing—evaluation's gold standard—NFP's stunning results for both mother and child speak eloquently for themselves. Of 46 early childhood programs studied by the Coalition for Evidence-Based Policy, NFP is one of only two meeting the "Top Tier" criteria of producing "sizeable, sustained benefits to participants and/or society." To name a few:

- Reduced healthcare encounters including injuries and emergency room visits
- 48% reduction in state-verified reports of child abuse and neglect
- 50% reduction in language delays
- 67% reduction in behavioral and emotional problems of children at age 6
- 59% reduction in arrests
- 90% reduction in adjudication as PINS (person in need of supervision) for incorrigible behavior
- Increase in mother's labor force and/or educational participation

Equally important to policy makers are the cost savings: The RAND Corporation reports that, for every dollar a community invests in NFP, they can see up to $5.70 in return.

A study published in the August 2015 issue of *Prevention Science* by Ted Miller, PhD, principal research scientist with the Pacific Institute for Research and Evaluation, reviewed evaluation findings, applied the impact estimates to the measured outcomes of 177,517 NFP clients—low-income pregnant women who were enrolled from 1996 to 2013. His study projects that, by 2031, NFP will prevent an estimated:

- 500 infant deaths
- 10,000 preterm births
- 13,000 dangerous closely-spaced second births
- 42,000 child maltreatment incidents
- 36,000 intimate partner violence incidents
- 90,000 violent crimes by youth
- 594,000 property and public order crimes (e.g., vandalism, loitering) by youth
- 36,000 youth arrests and
- 431,000 cases of youth substance abuse

NPF has made a major impact on both the lives of the most fragile, and on state and federal policy. The Maternal, Infant and Early Childhood Visiting (MIECHV) program is part of the Social Security Act, which includes the Maternal and Child Health Block Grant. MIECHV requires states to establish and meet specified child health, education and economic sufficiency benchmarks as a condition of receiving federal funding. MIECHV provides grants to the states for early visiting programs. NFP is among the few "eligible" programs on which states can spend federal money. NFP has received ringing endorsements from mayors such as Michael Bloomberg, governors, leading non-profits and top research institutions.

Driving the Statistics: The Relational

NFP adheres to an instructional curriculum for the health of both mother and child. Nurses provide a lot of "nurse-type" advice such as checking vital signs, advising on medical care, diet, smoking and alcohol, and helping to train for the arrival of a new baby. But that doesn't seem to lie at the heart of NFP. NFP provides first-time expectant mothers with a relationship they can count on.

"I tell the nurses that they are the unconditional listeners, the one positive voice. Most of these first-time moms are trashed, told they are lazy, irresponsible or just not given any guidance. These nurses may be the only nurturer the mothers have ever met."

-Mary Beth Haas, Nurse Supervisor Team I, NFP, Philadelphia, PA

Building trust with young women who have not experienced trust and who live in mistrusting neighborhoods is an essential aspect of the work. "Oh, we stalk them, we won't let them go," said Haas. Others cited praise, listening, presence, persistence, and follow through as trust builders. "Trust is fragile with fragile people. Trust can be broken in a minute," said another.

Formal evaluations cannot capture this. How does one quantify a vital, even loving relationship where moms can be radically vulnerable, know what it means to be safe, and, at the same time, delighted by progress, progress they can share with someone who knows on the deepest level what it means. I think of my own daughter, (the world's best mother, of course), in New York City, calling with reports both thrilling and vexing about her one-year-old—"Guess what: I think he said 'Papa' today." "He has a favorite book, and he knows which one it is!" Or the troubling: "What happened? He reverted to soft foods. It's so frustrating. He threw the solid food on the floor. What am I doing wrong?"

How does a formal evaluation capture what Samia and Nafessa said? "I wanted her to be proud of me. I was excited to show her something new," said Samia. "And she encouraged me, giving me confidence that I could do it. Julie [an NFP nurse] opened a new door for me." Samia now serves as a peer counselor.

"Julie is the only person who told me I could do something. She believed in me. She wanted to grow with me. She gave me confidence," remarked Nafessa. How does one quantify the power of having faith in another? And the exponential value in accepting, recognizing and believing in that faith—and, perhaps, believing in oneself? Nafessa's comments jolted me. I realized that something so profoundly important and life changing—one person's belief in another causing the other to believe in themselves—is rarely if ever recorded by our research. Undetected, but essential to the outcomes we try so hard to measure.

Impact on Nurses

NFP nurses seem to love this particular branch of nursing. "It's not routine. You knock on the door and you never know what's inside. It's always new. We have to think on our feet. We tailor our response to each individual client," said one NFP nurse. The nurses thrill at the prospect of "having a hand in the future of both mother and child." Nurses see their success rooted in being "radically respectful," both teaching and co-shaping the future with the young mothers. Gordon MacDougall, President of Beacon Associates, long an advocate and supporter of NFP and early liaison between NFP and the federal government puts it succinctly: "The secret sauce of NFP is motivation—young first-time mothers wanting a better life for their children and trusting relationships with nurses who care."

The work is not easy. NFP nurses carry a caseload of about 25 mothers whom they visit weekly for the first few months, then taper off, every few weeks, then monthly. They stay with the moms for two years. Most young mothers with whom nurses work face a cascade of issues that have little to do with nursing—lack of food, abusive or absent boyfriends, lack of access to school or jobs, living in high crime areas, and more, or as Nafessa put it, "everything." Finding and connecting moms to essential resources such as food stamps, drug abuse counseling, or GED programs then becomes a significant part of the work. And sometimes the work is dangerous. One nurse was jumped on her way to a mother living in a rough neighborhood. Because of the trusting relationship, further problems were avoided. "But," said Julie, an NFP nurse, "she called to tell me a few days later, informing me that things were 'hot' in her neighborhood. She said, 'Don't come into the neighborhood today.' You see, they protect us."

Weekly supervision sessions help nurses share successes, disappointments and problems, sometimes their own pain. "Most important," said one young nurse, "we are a community. We have each other."

The pay for NFP nurses is less than their counterparts who work in hospitals or clinics. And funding is always an issue as federal/state funding never covers all costs. So a significant part of the work involves raising money from city, philanthropic, corporate and individual sources. But mission overrides everything. Erin Graham, an NFP nurse supervisor, noted that, "Many of the moms call even after two years wanting to tell me how their kids are doing."

"This is the job I've wanted all my life. This is everything I've wanted to do in nursing. My clients give to me as much as I give to them. This work is so inspiring. I get to witness changed lives," beamed Joy Ahn.

RESOURCES

- Nurse-Family Partnership –
  (http://www.nursefamilypartnership.org/)
- The Center for the Study of Prevention of Violence –
  (http://www.Colorado.edu/cspv/blueprints)
- The Prevention Institute - *Preventing Violence: A Primer*
  (http://www.preventioninstitute.org/)

POLICY WALKING

CHAPTER 3

From Trauma to Triumph:

Becoming a Man and Working on Womanhood

"My brother was shot and killed. I don't know anything about my dad. I was angry every day. Ready to hit someone or worse. No more. I'm going to college. I'm going to be a cornerback."

- 10th grade boy, Bowen High School,

participant in Becoming a Man (BAM)

POLICY

The U.S. spends well over $500 billion annually on K-12 public schools, primarily to develop academic skills (U. S. Census Bureau, 2010). Yet very little attention is given to other important "determinants of student success," namely "social-cognitive skills." These skills include things like self-control, conflict resolution, future orientation, and social information processing, according to a University of Chicago study. Simply put: if I'm too angry, too scared, too preoccupied, or too quick to fight at the slightest provocation, I cannot learn. As one youth counselor told me, "You see, Mr. Calhoun, we just can't get our kids out of Viet Nam."

WALKING

"My dad's in jail. I never know what my mother's going to do. Or even where she's going to be. My world shakes every day. But WOW is my anchor. I never would have even thought about graduation without WOW. I would never have even dreamed of college. Me. Me? My brain couldn't have even gotten to dream because I was worried all the time. I never would have thought about how good I can be. Now I do. WOW saved me."

- 11th grade girl, Bowen High School, Chicago, IL, participant in Working on Womanhood (WOW)

Hard to believe this is not Syria or Iraq. It's Bowen High School on the south side of Chicago, close to the Illinois-Indiana border. The school's motto could adorn any high school in America: "All Bowen students and families will obtain an excellent education, compete globally and affect positive change in their communities." Other "mottos" hint at what Bowen faces: "Hopelessness ends here."

I was part of a federal site team visiting Chicago in late October 2014. Chicago is one of 15 cities participating in the National Forum on Youth Violence Prevention. We met with key staff, the mayor's deputies, Mayor Emanuel himself, school, law enforcement, health personnel, and faith-based and community organizations, all working tirelessly to stop the violence—in 2013 alone, Chicago experienced 415 homicides and 1,864 shootings. The next day, we took a long ride south to the city limits and Bowen High School to learn more about two programs that seemed to be the beginning of where hopelessness was ending.

Bowen. A school? Or a heavily guarded citadel? We started early, walking the school's periphery, talking to community members wearing uniforms as part of the city's safe passages program. "Juan, did you do your homework?" "Sarah, did you get breakfast this morning?" A warm, personal welcome for every kid. They knew every child by name. If a child had not eaten that morning, the safe passage workers send a quick walkie talkie message from the street to the school. "Sarah needs breakfast." School? A metal detector? Electronic screening guarding access to class? Yes. This is Bowen High School.

But then you're in. Posters adorn the halls. One is greeted, welcomed. Kids seem, well, like kids. The programs, classes really, Becoming a Man (BAM) and Working on Womanhood (WOW), "have made a huge difference," said Nia Abdullah, Bowen's principal. "I used to be so excited going to school when I was a child. All clean and dressed. Excited. I was always so eager to share what I learned with my parents. This is so different. Kids are afraid to go to school. Most of them cannot depend on breakfast, or books or book bags, or even clean clothes." But it's changing. The high school graduation rate is up, crime is down, school suspensions are down, and the kids seem proud to attend. Bowen, once a pariah school."

BAM—and a similar program for young women called WOW—*begin* with and *focus on* the socio-cognitive: self-control, conflict resolution, future orientation, and social information processing. At their core, these programs are a type of therapy called cognitive behavior therapy. "But if we called it that, we'd have nobody sitting in those chairs," says Marshaun Bacon, MSW, BAM Senior Curriculum Specialist. "Kids have a very biased view of therapy," continues Bacon, "They are so defensive that when someone mentions therapy, they think, 'Now somebody's calling me crazy.' So it's about a journey—how to become a man. How to become a woman. It's about future, and that's rare because for these kids, it's all about tonight, or even this afternoon."

BAM and WOW participants meet once a week for the entire school year. Youth in the programs are given time out from regular classes to attend the BAM and WOW groups, which blend counseling, impulse control, self-regulation, recognition of social cues (what sets the youth off or 'triggers' them) and development of a sense of personal responsibility and integrity.

And it works. BAM is one of very few such programs in the nation whose impact has been rigorously evaluated. BAM is not just hopeful, not just promising—it is a program that works, a program whose participants were measured against a comparison group—a group that did not participate in BAM—in a "randomized controlled trial" of the sort that provides "gold-standard" evidence in medicine. The first rigorous evaluation found that BAM, "strengthened social-cognitive skills and generated *massive* declines in violent crimes by at-risk youth," reported the University of Chicago Crime Lab, which has been studying BAM since 2009.

BAM began in 2001, and WOW was developed several years later by Youth Guidance: Guiding Kids to Bright Futures, an agency with years of experience and deep expertise running similar groups with girls. Anthony Ramirez-DiVittorio, MA, LCPC, BAM Training Manager and Founder, notes that the counselors also "become vulnerable" during the meetings, helping to "create a safe space." I asked him where the idea for BAM came from, its genesis: "I was a street kid with a strong mom," he responds. Armed with a clinical degree, he began working as a counselor in a middle-school setting. He found himself borrowing from his different experiences, "a little clinical work, some education, some service work, some mentoring." A tile here, a tile there but no overall mosaic—yet. At one point, it struck Tony that he was on a Carl Rogers path, Rogers probably 20th century America's most influential psychologist. Rogers pioneered the "self-actualization" movement, asserting that, to grow and thrive, young people needed an environment that allowed for self-disclosure, acceptance, and empathy.

Citing Rogers, Anthony said, "Then it hit me—this work is all about these kids growing up, becoming men. Not," he stressed, "being a man, but *becoming* a man. It's a constant, transformative process." Thus, BAM began to take shape.

Hugs and Tears

While the weekly group meeting lies at BAM's heart, a safe place where things can be shared, respect is required and accountability is modeled and practiced, what goes on outside is where the values and behaviors are tested, actualized. "A kid can tell us he's having a hard time focusing on his school work," says Tony. "Then he might focus in the circle, listening well, asking good questions, helping. Then we say, 'Wow, you are really focused!' How are you going to keep that focus outside of the circle? How can you apply it to your classwork?'" The emotional "heart work" connects them to the clinical, the behaviorist side. For example, offers Tony, "I might say to a kid, 'based on your anger now, what choice are you going to make after school?'" He continues, "You see, these kids are always told 'don't do drugs,' 'finish high school,' 'don't carry a gun,' but it's never actualized. Nobody's helping them with the actual choices. You can't just talk at them. You've got to see the volcano first, and then ask, 'What are you going to do with all of that?'"

In addition to the circle, BAM stresses service, "engagement," encouraging BAM youth to see themselves as helpers, as important role models for others. Included among BAM's engagement strategies are outside trips to colleges, museums, concerts, and sports events.

I attended both a BAM and WOW session. Hugs and tears closed both sessions. Sessions are highly structured. The groups begin with each participant "checking in," sharing his or her thoughts and feelings following a PIES format; a safe space to share what's going on along four dimensions:

Physically:	*"I'm really tired today because there was too much noise at home."*
Intellectually:	*"I've got so many things going on in my head, but I'm excited because I think two*

	colleges are interested in me because of my running."
Emotionally:	"I'm really having a hard time because I'm changing and my old friends never let up on me. I'm so lonely. You guys are all I've got."
Spiritually:	"I know God is with me." Or, as one youth told me, "There is no God because if there was I wouldn't be in this mess."

After the check-ins, the discussion assumes a life of its own, with a lesson interrupted at times by students turning to help one another or to clarify or to support their peers. The BAM counselor keeps tabs on anything that comes up during the discussion that would warrant a follow-up conversation with a student, a teacher, or school counselor. There is such openness, such raw pain, such vulnerability that closing with a hug at the end of the session seems a (and perhaps the only) natural conclusion. "This is a head and heart program, and it's about the only place they seem comfortable," says Marshaun, "the only place they're not on guard."

Principal Abdullah reports a "huge difference…fewer incidents, fewer disciplines, increase in graduation rates. And less crime. And the school atmosphere is totally different."

Fight or Flight

Most homicides, most shootings are unplanned—they are often impulsive, hair-trigger responses to perceived slights, made lethal because of the availability of a firearm. Mass shootings—San Bernardino, Newtown, Columbine—dominate the mainstream news media, but these are but a tiny percentage of our national gun violence problem. The daily toll of gun violence in communities in Chicago and elsewhere rarely makes the front pages: one lost life in this neighborhood, two in that neighborhood, and, before long, you have more than one murder every single day in cities across America. Pretty soon, we reach a number not matched by all our wars.

Fight or flight is a daily reality for young people at schools like Bowen. Most of these youth exhibit some form of PTSD. For many, violence is a constant presence in their lives. Most have witnessed shootings, some homicides. BAM and WOW seek to slow down the students' hair-trigger responses in high-stakes situations, helping provide a glimpse of future beyond tomorrow and support, support, support.

A.J. Watson, BAM Director, underscores the program's core values:

Integrity – *I am a man of my word. My values equal my actions.*

Accountability – *I am responsible for the consequences of my actions, whether intended or unintended.*

Self-Determination – *I pursue my goals in the face of adversity.*

Positive Anger Expression – *I learn that anger is a normal emotion that needs to be expressed. How I express my anger is a choice, whether as a savage or as a warrior.*

Respect for Womanhood – *I am more mindful and respectful in how I interact with women.*

Visionary Goal Setting – *I create a vision for myself and who I am, how I want to be seen in the world. I set goals based on my vision and make responsible choices that help me achieve these goals.*

I asked A.J. what keeps him on this path, how he stays on it. He first described his own epiphany while consulting with a charter school network on the U.S./Mexico border, where he witnessed the impact a well-run school could have: "I saw the impact on kids, their families and the community. I knew then that I wanted to use my MBA and my business and analytical skills to help young men of color in a transformative way and in a school setting." But it's not just the kids who've been transformed. "Because of BAM. I've become more open, more vulnerable." He's looked harder at the choices he's making and will make, realizing "*I am still becoming a man. Because of BAM I am a better husband and a better father. BAM has transformed me.*"

A Better Future by the Numbers

The University of Chicago's Crime Lab initially evaluated the program after selecting BAM through a design competition it held soon after it was launched in 2008. A careful 'social autopsy' the Crime Lab carried out that year had "revealed that a large share of homicides of Chicago youth stem from impulsive behavior—young people with access to guns, massively over-reacting to some aspect of their social environment. This finding is consistent with a growing body of research showing that 'social-cognitive' skills such as impulse control, future orientation, and conflict resolution are predictive of a wide range of key life outcomes." Building on these findings, the Crime Lab held a design competition to select a promising program for a rigorous evaluation. In a more recent study of BAM, the Crime Lab offers insight into the mechanisms behind the program's success, finding that BAM seems to work in part by helping youth to slow down and behave less automatically in high stakes situations. The result? High value outcomes:

- The original Crime Lab study (conducted during the 2009-10 academic year) projected that positive impacts of BAM on school engagement would result in a 10 to 23% increase in high school graduation rates relative to the control group.

·• BAM also reduced violent crime arrests for students in the program by a stunning 44%.

The Becoming a Man (BAM) and Working on Womanhood (WOW) programs are supported by a mix of public and private funding. This includes revenue from Chicago Public Schools, the U.S. Department of Education and a diverse mix of corporate, philanthropic, and individual support. The program costs about $2,300 per participant, but research suggests that the benefits far outweigh the modest program costs: "If these graduation impacts are realized, the resulting social benefits would be on the order of $49,000 to $119,000 per participant from increased lifetime earnings, tax payments and lower public benefit use" (See White House Council of Economic Advisers report on ROI, pg. 23, listed below).

The White House Council of Economic Advisers concludes:

"Given how little policy attention is currently devoted to improving social-cognitive skills of disadvantaged youth, there may be considerable returns to society from expanding investments in this area."

One of the BAM boys gave me a much less policy-laden conclusion: "If it weren't for BAM I wouldn't be aiming for college." "What would you be doing?" I asked. "I wouldn't be doing. I'd be dead."

RESOURCES

- Youth Guidance (www.youth-guidance.org/BAM)
- The University of Chicago – Crime Lab BAM Report (https://crimelab.uchicago.edu/page/becoming-man-BAM-sports-edition-findings)
- The University of Chicago – Social Service Administration (https://ssa.uchicago.edu/becoming-man)
- White House Council of Economic Advisers Report: *"Economic Costs of Youth Disadvantage and High-Return Opportunities for Change"* (see page 23) (https://www.whitehouse.gov/sites/default/files/docs/mbk_repo rt_final_update1.pdf)

CHAPTER 4

The Overlooked Partner:

Youth as Resources

"The best way to find yourself is to lose yourself in the service of others."

- Gandhi

It was about 7:00 at night many years ago when the call came through. "Jack, is it you? Do you remember me?" That voice, slow, measured, deep. I hadn't heard it in about 10 years. Familiar, yes, but I couldn't yet anchor it in a person. "Keep talking," I said. I heard the voices of young children in the background. "I know I know you, but I can't recall your name!" "Jack, it's Donnie Hinkle." Donnie was calling from home.

His face, his situation flashed before me as if written in bold letters on a large page. Donnie Hinkle: a sullen probationer from Indianapolis who had enrolled in the Youth as Resources (YAR) program, an initiative I launched as President and CEO of the National Crime Prevention Council. Donnie, who with others, helped to rebuild an entire playground, a playground he had earlier helped to trash.

Begun in the late 1980s, YAR thrived for almost 25 years, spreading throughout the country, involving roughly 400,000 youth. Other local organizations and national organizations have adopted YAR, or its core principles, and two of the very first continue to thrive, one in Evansville, IN, and the other under the aegis of the United Way in Indianapolis.

POLICY

What's our message to youth, what's our promise? We seem to be good at predicting and preparing for failure, standing, waiting for the bad to happen, and then when it does, swift and very expensive interventions. Our reigning models are deficit models. Approaches to youth resting solely on the pathological won't work.

Our august policy discussions identify teen problems—teen pregnancy, child abuse, violence, drug abuse, dropping out of school. But they often miss the very heart of the problem—the aloneness, the isolation, the disconnection of youth from that which makes society work: family, school, community, job, and a sense of future. The gaping hole for many of today's youth is the lack of a sense of place in the community and a stake therein, and, if poor, they also feel they have little to give, little anyone wants or needs.

The absence of such bonding strikes at the very heart of what it means to be a person, which is, in part, beholden-ness to others. It also strikes at the very heart of our political structure, for, if teens do not view themselves as subscribing to the social contract, they will see no sense in following it.

When serving as CEO of the National Crime Prevention Council, I commissioned the Harris Organization to poll youth about ways in which crime and violence influenced their lives. Half the news was old, i.e., that because of crime, kids occasionally carried weapons, cut classes, dropped out. But the astounding new news was that 9 out of 10 said they would volunteer to do something about crime and violence and community improvement if only they knew what to do.

In a world rife with fragmented families and anonymous neighborhoods, youth need opportunities to give, to bind themselves positively to the community, to try on adult roles, to become contributing citizens. The community needs to send the message that youth are needed, their views and skills valued. All youth ache to belong, to feel needed, that he or she can make important contributions. Youth policy typically clusters in five areas: education; family and child welfare; job training, retraining and school-to-work policies; health and remediation; and responses to juvenile crime. As such, in our darker moments, we tend to view youth as packages of pathologies ready to explode, not as resources to be engaged. We need the best in healers, those who would counsel, mentor, provide job training, but we also must figure out ways to make youth feel connected, needed, that they have something of value to give. The opposite of "disconnection" is not fixing, which may be needed, but "connection," passionate involvement, which broadens our definition of good from being good, which we usually tell youth, to actively doing good.

WALKING

I started Teens as Community Resources in the late 1970s when flying back and forth from DC to Boston to finish my Masters in Public Administration from Harvard's Kennedy School of Government. John Ramsey, also a mid-career student and program officer at the Boston Foundation, and I designed it on a napkin at a bar in Cambridge. As head of Justice Resource Institute and later as Commissioner of Youth Services, I had started a program for delinquent youth to give something back either to their victims or to the community. It had worked. Why not focus it on preventing delinquency rather than addressing it after the fact? "It's time," I recall saying, "we stopped fixing teens and started claiming them." The program took off. Later, under the aegis of the National Crime Prevention Council, Youth as Resources as it became known, spread like wildfire in Indiana with major support from the Lilly Endowment, and subsequently was picked up by the foundation community in cities throughout the United States. By the year 2000, almost 400,000 youth were served—no, roughly 400,000 youth served.

YAR rooted itself in the belief that youth needed to be involved, connected, invited to partner with adults. Its core concept could not have been simpler: YAR asks youth to spot social issues about which they are concerned, and then design a program to address those concerns. Youth would have to write a proposal and apply for a mini-grant, arguing their case before a youth-led/adult-involved board.

YAR is not a program run by adults: it is a youth-driven program with adults as partners. YAR's potency rests on the fact that all youth have something to give, particular talents they can use to address a concern of theirs. Thus, the jock can help to coach, the artist can create brochures and murals on AIDS, the singer rap songs, the dancers create a modern dance on peer pressure, and the talker mediate disputes.

Typically in a participating city, a YAR board comprises those who work with and care about youth (schools, youth workers, the United Way, churches, Boys and Girls Clubs, etc.) is set up. The board disseminates requests for proposals and then screens responses, awarding mini-grants in the $100 to $5,000 range depending on local grant guidelines. Youth sit on, and sometimes chair, the boards. The results have been striking:

- Youth have tackled all kinds of issues about which communities are concerned such as drug abuse, hunger, homelessness, pollution, lonely elderly, violence. Thousands of teen-led programs were created.
- The beneficiaries—from kids tutored, elderly helped, houses built, plays enacted, disputes settled—are too numerous to count.

- At its high point, YAR existed in 42 states and 11 countries.
- All types of youth have participated, from the delinquent to the honor society student.
- Youth from the widest variety of entities seek YAR grants—schools, churches, youth clubs, probation, child welfare, service agencies.
- Many of these agencies subsequently changed policies to incorporate a youth-in-service dimension.
- Troubled, disconnected youth have found connection and belonging, sometimes through their own pain: pregnant teens writing and acting in a play about the burdens of being a teen mom; incarcerated boys visiting high schools, sharing the results of their poor choices.

Youth who signed up for YAR originally tended to be the leaders, the confident, the connected. But would it work with the disconnected, too, those on society's edge, those in foster care, in the juvenile justice system, even homeless kids? It did.

Results

Formal studies of YAR-involved youth showed increases in self-esteem, competence, and empathy, an enduring belief in the value of service and some educational gains. A comparative evaluation of the Michigan Community Foundation's youth project initiative found that youth:

- Felt like they were making a difference
- Learned about community needs
- Learned leadership skills
- Developed positive relationships with other teens and adults
- Had career plans positively affected

Evaluating the YAR program in Indiana, PSL Associates and Glancy Associates found:

- Increase in self esteem
- Increase in confidence
- Expanded horizons
- For incarcerated youth (Indiana Girls School and Indiana Boys School), less recidivism, fewer incidents, more ambitious career goals
- Change in concept of time: from nothing beyond this afternoon or tomorrow to a future of which they are a part

The research is clear: youth who engage in service, youth who volunteer experience better outcomes. UCLA Higher Education Research Institute found that youth who volunteer are more likely to do well in school, graduate, vote and be philanthropic. According to the Search Institute, youth who volunteer just one hour or more a week are 50 percent less likely to abuse drugs, alcohol, cigarettes, or engage in other destructive behavior.

YAR made an extraordinary impact, especially in the State of Indiana:

- In 1997 YAR received the statewide "Unsung Heroes" Award from the University of Indiana's Center on Philanthropy.
- In 1998, YAR's throughout the state received the "Blueprint Award" from the Indiana Youth Institute for "Exemplifying the principles of healthy development for children and youth in Indiana."
- In 2005, Youth Resource (Evansville) was selected as the overall winner of Indiana Achievement Award in the Impact Category for how its programs improved and impacted the community.
- In November 2005, Evansville was awarded the prestigious distinction from Colin Powell's America's Promise as one of the 100 Best Communities for Young People.

Why YAR Works: Uncovering Resiliency

You need adults willing to help with logistics, treating youth as if they have brains and helping with "adult things" like transportation, opening a bank account, renting a truck, meeting times that work for busy youth, providing pizza (teens are always hungry), and celebrating success. You need a flexible, tolerant adult willing to cede some adult power, let youth make a few mistakes, involve youth in governance, and then make sure youth get credit—lots of it.

But why YAR really works is because it taps into youth resiliency. The literature on resiliency, on youth who succeed, reference many factors. Five stand out:

- A locus of control. They do not feel blown around randomly by the winds of fate. They have a goal, whether modest such as improving a grade or large such as attending medical school.
- A skill to which they can point—playing an instrument, singing, running a meeting, playing basketball.
- A trusted adult who is there no matter what, no matter how severe the existential tornado. That adult can be a parent, a relative, a teacher, a coach, or a mentor.
- Optimism, defined either in a secular way (hope for the future) or theologically ("He holds me in the palm of His hand.")
- Altruism – "I am my brother's/sister's keeper."

Examples of purpose-empowered youth abound. One young woman who volunteered to work in a shelter for battered women said, "I want them to get the love that I never got as a child." I recall speaking with Earl at a large, public fair where YAR participants showcased their projects. Earl, a probationer, was a large, cross-eyed boy with a large scar running down one cheek. He proudly described his project, designed with his fellow probationers, a project where the participants helped elderly shut-ins with various tasks such as mowing the lawn or reading to them. "Earl," I said, "if I were 85 years old and you came in to read to me, I'd jump out the window! You are one big, tough-looking guy." "You don't understand," replied Earl, "It's the first time I've ever been thanked."

For many teens, the future is later today or tomorrow. Envisioning future means hope and participation in that future. One young woman whose team helped hack through brush to build an environmental trail said, "My grandchildren will see this and be able to use it."

Another powerful lesson YAR learned, epiphanies really—youth discovering skills they never knew they possessed. At one YAR awards ceremony held in the lobby of the Hyatt Indianapolis, a local TV personality who served as master of ceremonies called out the names of the project "leads." He had no idea who was who, who was a class president or who had been locked up at the Indiana Girls School, a female prison. He called up the next YAR lead, Melissa and her project, "Soup's On." He asked her about her project. "We cook for the homeless. We use a recipe I got from my mother," she responded. "Great," said the host, "How did you feel about your project?" Melissa paused. "At first I felt awful." "Awful?" exclaimed the stunned host. "Yes," she responded. "I realized I have so much and the homeless have so little." So much: Melissa, a victim of sexual abuse, Melissa involved with drugs, Melissa a school dropout. She looked up at the host before she left the stage, saying, "I feel good because I realize how much I have to give."

A surprise: empathy. The need to give begins early. Second graders in New York's PS 163 decided they should feed the homeless who were harassing them en route to school. "Feeding them is not enough," said one young child. "They need more than that. Let's put love notes in the bags with the food." Teachers reported that some of the homeless helped to escort the kids to school.

And finally, Tanika Reilly, a resident of one of the most violent public housing projects in America, Chicago's Robert Taylor Homes, which were subsequently torn down. Tanika's gift is singing. Nine-year-old Tanika and her classmates designed a program where they would sing to the elderly walled in by crime. Tanika, whose mother seemed almost an adolescent herself, faced a daily gauntlet of trouble: sleeping in a bathtub to avoid gunfire; wending her way to school trying to avoid gangs and stepping on condoms and crack vials. Yet when she received a YAR mini-grant to support her project she pulled the mic down to where she could reach it, saying, "Thank you for allowing me to make my community better."

Regardless of the project, the real accomplishment for these kids is forging a connection and purpose—and being appreciated, a sense that they are important and needed, that they have something to give. And through YAR, adults communicate a profound message: "You are part of us. We cannot solve these problems without you."

Thus our task: believe that the spark is there (it is): elicit it, nurture it, celebrate it, and, if possible, sustain it. I've always wondered whether Tanika's spark still glows. Statistics would say otherwise: more than 60 percent of young women growing up in her zip code will have borne a child out of wedlock, and a similar percentage of the young men will have wound up in the criminal justice system—probation, parole or corrections. Many will have been killed.

This nation has a huge resource waiting to be asked to help. Youth, millions of them ready to raise their hands, many including the Donnie Hinkles of America.

> *"Jack. You remember you came to our group home. You said you wanted to try an experiment. You said you wanted to prove that kids who had gotten into trouble could prove to the community and themselves that they were valuable. Don't you remember?"*
>
> *I remembered. I had not spent much time with Donnie in my entire life, probably about six hours: two to three hours working on the dream with those in the group home, the*

courts and the probation department, and then months later at a press conference where a stunningly beautiful, complicated, brightly colored playground was unveiled.

"Donnie, of course I remember. But why are you calling?"

"Jack, I had a bad life." He recounted his grim story. "You were one of only two people who had faith in me. Two: you and my mentor who stuck with me in the group home. See, Jack, you had such faith in me that I started to have faith in myself. And when I built that playground, and all those people congratulated me, I knew I could do good things in my life."

"Jack," he continued, "I'm starting as an iron worker at the Indianapolis Airport next Monday at $23.00 an hour. I'm in the Iron Workers Union. I wanted to find you to thank you."

"For what, Donnie?" I replied, "It was you, not me."

RESOURCES

I have focused on one particular youth in service project, Youth as Resources. YAR is but one model among many initiatives that would harness the energies of our young people. Among them are:

- The National League of Cities, Institute for Youth, Education and Families (http://www.nlc.org/iyef) especially its publication "Promoting Youth Participation," which cites the many ways cities have harnessed the energies of youth, e.g., Youth Councils, Youth Mapping, Mayor's Youth Councils, The National Crime Prevention Council, Teens, Crime and the Community (http://www.ncpc.org/portal_vocabularies/ncpcprograms/teens-crime-and-the-community-tcc)
- Two programs in Indiana: Youth Resources, Evansville, Indiana (http://www.youth-resources.org) and Youth as

Resources, Central Indiana
(http://www.uwci.org/programs/youth-as-resources).

- Extensive information about YAR can be found at
http://www.HopeMatters.org
- National Network for Youth (http://www.nn4youth.org)
promotes the positive development of youth through
community and youth involvement on governing boards and
other decision-making bodies.
- America's Promise (http://americaspromise.org) and Youth
Service America (http://www.ysa.org): YSA is the premier
alliance of more than 200 organizations committed to
increasing the quantity and quality of opportunities for
young Americans to serve.
- The Corps Network (http://www.corpsnetwork.org) provides
participants with job training, academic programming,
leadership skills, and additional support through a strategy of
services that improves communities and the environment.
- The Corporation for Nation Services
(http://www.nationalservice.gov/americorps) provides young
people the opportunity to serve via AmeriCorps/Vista.
- Kids at Hope (http://kidsathope.org) is a national youth
development organization that studies family, school and
community culture to better understand the dynamics that
lead to success or failure.
- National Citizen Service (UK)
(http://www.ncsyes.co.uk/about-ncs)
- "Say Y.E.S. To Youth: Youth Engagement Strategies:"
(http://extension.psu.edu/publications/agrs-098) offers
benefits of adult/youth partnerships, discusses strategies for
sustaining youth interest and provides practical assessment
and engagement forms.

CHAPTER 5

Aiming Policy at Reducing Gun Violence:
It Starts Closest to the Pain

"I've already picked out the dress I'll wear when I'm in a casket."
- Young woman in Oakland, California

Prayer groups are intimate. Here, the broken heart seeks healing, meaning. Here, pain and vulnerabilities are shared, and hearts and hands embrace to comfort, to soothe.

On June 17, 2015, a murderer walked into this place of healing. The Emanuel AME Church in Charleston subscribes to the most fundamental of biblical precepts: "You shall also love the stranger, for you were strangers in the land of Egypt" (Deut: 10:19). Dylann Roof, a stranger, was welcomed by the Mother Emanuel Bible study and prayer group. He was given a chair in the healing circle. Roof then slaughtered nine members who stretched out their arms to welcome him.

Safe places, surely schools? No. Sandy Hook. Columbine. Safe places, surely a movie theater or a business? No. Aurora. A shopping mall in Minneapolis. Safe places, surely churches? No.

The 2015 murders in a church in Charleston, S.C., brought home the grim reality, once again, that a nation awash in guns has no safe haven—not even a church.

POLICY

For the most part, U.S. crime statistics look much the same as other western nations—that is until guns enter the equation. 30,000 gun deaths per year. No other developed nation comes close. Some cities show breathtaking drops in homicides: New York City recorded 2,245 homicides in 1990 and only 237 in 2012; Los Angeles reported 1092 homicides in 1992 and 298 in 2012. Stunning and laudable plunges. Should we cheer? Combined, Britain, Australia and Canada see fewer than 350 gun-related murders per year. Non-gun related suicide rates are consistent across the rest of the developed world. Factor in firearms and the U.S. suicide rate doubles.

The NRA claims guns make us safe. But the statistics say otherwise. States with the most lax gun laws show proportionately higher gun deaths. And the converse is true: Strong gun control laws, fewer deaths. Civic and governmental leaders in the nation's largest cities believe they have done all they can to reduce gun deaths through prevention measures, intervention strategies, gun buybacks, targeting the most notorious offenders and more, but most assert that they cannot go further unless state and national gun laws change. California, with the strongest gun laws in the nation, reduced firearm mortality rates by an astonishing 56 percent between 1993 and 2010. And law-abiding gun owners still have their guns.

The Double Standard of Danger: Attacking the "Agent"

Our leaders are assiduous about protecting us. The FDA intends to ban trans-fats such as coffee creamer and similar products that "clog arteries." Sudden Infant Death Syndrome triggered the recall and redesign of cribs. Tainted spinach, which caused a handful of deaths and sickened many people, was pulled from the shelves. Cars with defective brakes are instantly recalled. Seat belts and air bags, required, have saved thousands of lives. The essence of the public health approach is to address the core of the problem, to attack the "agent," clean up tainted water, get rid of flea infested rats, immunize against measles and polio.

But when it comes to guns, there are no such protections. With guns, we do the opposite: spend all our resources after the crisis: we've become quicker in our response time after a shooting; we're becoming much more adept at saving gunshot victims, and we are superb at grief counseling, and trauma-based care for those who witness gun violence. All of these interventions have become a standard part of our response. But to go after the "agent"—the gun—no.

"It's people, not guns, who kill," proclaim many. Okay, then what would happen if we have thorough background checks for "people," in addition to training and licensing as we do for driver's licenses, and ban civilian ownership of weapons only the military should carry? The evidence is clear. States enacting even modest gun laws have recorded fewer gun deaths.

On Monday, August 2, 2015, the Major Cities Chiefs Association cited an alarming rise in gun deaths, unveiling a survey showing that police in many cities across the country "are seeing more guns on the streets and more killings" (*Washington Post*, 9/4/2015, p. B 1). "We felt a sense of urgency because people are dying," said D.C. Police Chief Cathy Lanier, one of the conference organizers. The chiefs cited the "proliferation of guns" as a central issue and recommended "more stringent gun laws, including harsher penalties for gun crimes and the use of high capacity magazines" (ibid.).

It seems that the further politicians are removed from the problem, the less willing they are to act, the more vulnerable they are to moneyed political pressure. Congress refuses to act. A few state legislatures have acted. But those closest to the pain—the mayors, city counselors, police, and local citizens who hear cries of grieving mothers and school officials who see the empty classroom seat of a slain youth—they have begun to act.

In the face of fierce opposition from gun rights groups, Los Angeles Mayor Eric Garcetti on July 28, 2015, signed into law a ban on the possession of high-capacity ammunition magazines in his city. Such magazines have been the common thread in the nation's mass shootings.

But it may well be that children will lead us.

WALKING

Inner City Youth Leading the Way?

Counter to the grim statistics, a hopeful counter story exists, a story of a public health advocate in California in the 1980s who discovered that guns had become the number one killer of children in California. Twinning her public health background with her commitment to kids, she harnessed the energies of the most vulnerable youth, arming them with data which the youth linked to their own heartrending stories.

As she began her work, one young woman said, "I've already picked out the dress I'll wear when I'm in a casket." While most young girls were focused on what to wear to prom, these young women were making their funeral arrangements. Such stories stoked her passion and her mission: to train youth living in communities with the highest rates of violence to become youth educators and leaders to prevent gun violence. The result? A change in local gun ordinances and California's passage of the most stringent gun control laws in the nation.

It really wasn't a fair fight. Gun advocates underestimated my sister, Deane Calhoun, and her well-trained army of kids. First of all, she knew the numbers, even though statistics were hard to come by. The gun industry had put a chill on public agencies sharing any information that might be useful to preventing gun violence, and had gone so far as to pressure Congress to pass legislation barring the Centers for Disease Control from gathering and distributing statistics related to gun violence. The data arrived surreptitiously, sometimes just dropped off near her office door in a paper bag. Through her work in Oakland, she knew the kids. She believed in the kids. They wanted to put the numbers to work; they wanted to put the mortality and morbidity (death and injury) gun stats to work, to keep them from going up. They lived the statistics: almost all had heard about or seen someone shot or killed. Many had lost relatives to gun violence.

But she didn't want the youth to be tokens. She didn't want them to just read her material. She wanted them to write theirs. "No, we were partners, all the way. A team." She trained them in civics, in the legislative process, in how to speak, how to link their stories with the data. Keys to the unique collaboration included pizza, their belief in her, her belief in them, and rigorous training. It was academic— they were being trained in civic participation—but it was also highly personal. Another benefit: "Just our afterschool work together on the gun issue took kids off the streets, out of harm's way," said Deane. Many of them, for the first time in their lives, felt "heard," respected, that they had something important to give. They were on a mission.

Deane, as director of the non-profit, Youth ALIVE, also rounded up allies, letting others know how the gun issues affected their missions and must be addressed. For example, she taught philanthropists that violence stood between them and their quality education goals. In other words, they couldn't make an impact because violence, fear, and lack of safety, so negatively impacted a student's ability to learn. She brought in ministers who had buried one too many kids, police who felt outgunned, doctors seeing emergency rooms turning into MASH units, and city counselors from violence-plagued districts who were trying to protect kids, attempting to stop retaliatory shooting. She had allies, but her youth were the front line soldiers.

Youth soon discovered that their views about the reasons for gun violence echoed that of the most sophisticated research:

Kid-speak: *"Easy to get guns, drugs and alcohol."*
Research: *"Availability of guns, drugs and alcohol."*

Kid-speak: *"No jobs in our neighborhoods."*
Research: *"Relative economic disparity."*

The kids became walking translations of the research.

They went after the local paper, the *Oakland Tribune*, galvanized by an obit for a young gunshot victim adjacent to an advertisement for assault weapons for sale in a local gun store. Their pressure on the paper yielded little until Deane's team convinced the Oakland City Council to drop the *Tribune* as the Council's paper of record. The publisher gave in. He would advertise only sporting weapons.

When they began, the youth let Deane know that they could get a gun any time, any day, much more easily than they could get school supplies. Under-the-table "research" revealed that Oakland had 115 gun dealers, most operating out of their homes, most unregulated. In fewer than five years, there were none, as the youth, City Council, local citizens, non-profit agencies and the police, worked together to pass an ordinance banning residential gun dealers.

In the 1980s in California, guns were the leading killer of youth. As new assault rifles flooded the streets, a powerful multi-sector coalition supported what was then, and still is, the strongest assault gun ban in the country—California Senate Bill 23. This effort saved lives. By 2010 California's gun death rate had been cut by over half (56 percent) of the 1990 rate, reducing the state's gun deaths rate from fifteenth to forty-first among the fifty states, thus falling from above to below the national average (Law Center to Prevent Gun Violence. "The California Model: Twenty Years of Putting Safety First," July 29, 2013).

Some of those who testified in Sacramento were youth who spoke from wheelchairs, they themselves gunshot victims.

Deane showed that trained young people living in communities with the highest rates of gun violence could become peer educators and· leaders. The case study "Decreasing the Supply and Demand for Guns: Oakland's Youth Advocacy Project" summarized Youth ALIVE's success this way:

"Direct service organization's daily exposure to real-life client needs provides valuable insights for developing viable policies – plus highly motivated advocates. When backed by scientific findings on the causes of the problem, this synergy of youth participant engagement in civil society can promote good policy and build healthy communities."

It turned into a multi-decade process. The work was long and it was hard. What kept Deane going? "The kids! I knew them, their stories, their hope and that they would inspire. Almost every single one graduated from high school—in spite of a 49 percent high school drop-out rate in Oakland. Many attended college and most have jobs. I told them that I would never leave them for another job." The youth motivated Deane, kept her going.

"One night," reflects Deane, "when we had three city council meetings to attend, I was really flagging after the first two, and this after a 14-hour day. It was the kids who said: 'Deane, we gotta do it. We'll have fun, and we'll win.' They were right, every time. They motivated me, kept me going. Inspired me to never stop. I loved working with them."

Deane Calhoun won the California Peace Prize in 1995.

RESOURCES

- Youth ALIVE (http://www.youthalive.org): "Youth ALIVE is dedicated to preventing violence and developing youth leaders…."
- Calhoun, Deane, "Decreasing the Supply and Demand for Guns: Oakland's Youth Advocacy Project" Journal of Urban Health, Dec 2005, Volume 82, Issue 4, pp 552-559 (http://link.springer.com/article/10.1093/jurban/jti132)
- Law Center to Prevent Gun Violence (http://www.smartgunlaws.org) is a national law center that provides legal expertise in support of local and state gun violence prevention laws and local ordinances that save lives.
- States United to Prevent Gun Violence (http://www.ceasefireusa.org) is a provider of bi-weekly highlights of national and state gun violence prevention advocacy, research, news stories and citizen commentary.
- Violence Policy Center (http://www.vpc.org) is a national organization committed to research, advocacy, and education to reduce gun violence.
- Mayors Against Illegal Guns (http://www.everytown.org/mayors) is 5 million Americans working with lawmakers and community members to end gun violence and build safer communities through data-driven solutions.
- Sandy Hook Promise (http://sandyhookpromise.org) pledged to encourage and support sensible solutions to gun violence.
- The Brady Campaign Against Gun Violence (http://www.bradycampaign.org): The Brady Campaign works to pass and enforce state and federal gun laws, regulations, and public policies through activism, electing public officials who support common sense gun laws and public awareness strategies about gun violence.

CHAPTER 6

Skills + Service + Leadership + Love = YouthBuild's Stunning Success

"I used to be a menace to my community;
now I am a minister to it."

— YouthBuild Student

POLICY

Trouble follows those with little education and few marketable skills. Unable to participate in economic life, positive connections to a community's civic life weaken or disappear altogether. Thus, skill building and education become prime intervention strategies for individuals disconnected from civic and economic life. Linking skill building with service greatly improves the life trajectory for those on society's edge.

WALKING

"The main thing you have to understand is that they're not 'clients' or 'recipients of services.' They're students or constituents to whom we are accountable," explained Dorothy Stoneman, CEO and Founder, YouthBuild USA, Inc.

I met with Stoneman and three YouthBuild graduates, James Mackey (Columbus, OH), Lashon Amado (Brockton, MA), and

Anthony Williams (Boston, MA), for three hours on a rainy November day in 2015 at YouthBuild's headquarters in Somerville, Massachusetts.

Stoneman began YouthBuild in East Harlem in 1978, soon expanding it throughout the city, the state and then nationally and internationally. Through the program that provides training and education to unemployed young adults, 140,000 "students" have built 30,000 units of affordable housing since 1994. Two-hundred-and-sixty urban and rural YouthBuild sites now exist in 46 states in the USA. Through YouthBuild International, YouthBuild has been replicated by NGOs, government agencies, international development institutions and global companies in 102 communities in 15 countries.

YouthBuild's formally stated purpose, under the aegis of "A comprehensive Youth and Community Development Model," is "to break the cycle of poverty and unleash the positive energy of unemployed young adults to rebuild their communities and their own lives with a commitment to work, education, responsibility, community, and family." For unemployed young people who left high school without a diploma, YouthBuild provides the opportunity to reclaim their educations, gain the skills they need for employment, internalize the ethic of service, and become leaders in their communities.

The purpose statement and program description don't quite convey YouthBuild's essence. Stoneman's words do: "Know that our work goes well beyond transmitting skills. We train our leaders to participate in and value service, to improve communities, and to be leaders. Yes, we train. Yes, we provide education, but it's so much more. Love and respect are at the core of it. We believe in the power of love coupled with opportunity. Many of our students say, 'I came here for a GED, but what I found was a family.' One said, 'YouthBuild is like a windshield wiper. For the first time in a long time, I am able to see where I am heading.' Another said, 'I used to be a menace to my community; now I am a minister to it.'"

In one form or another, this work has been Dorothy's mission since she·joined the Civil Rights Movement through the Harlem Action Group in New York City after graduating from Harvard in 1963. Committed to helping young people who are eager to transcend the pain and despair of poverty and discrimination and contribute to social change so that others will not suffer or make the same mistakes that they have, she views her work in the context of eliminating poverty and injustice. She sits on many boards, has received many awards, and cites her invitation to speak at the 50th anniversary of the civil rights march on the National Mall, at which Dr. Martin Luther King Jr. delivered his "I Have a Dream" speech, as one of the highlights of her career.

YouthBuild's students emerge from situations that help shape YouthBuild's purpose and structure. All have grown up in poverty and almost all have left high school without a diploma, for a variety of reasons. Many have been entangled in the foster care and/or juvenile justice systems; many come from truly difficult family and community situations. Some are homeless, and many are already parents. A typical YouthBuild program is composed of 30-50 young people 16-24 years old, all of whom are low-income, 90 percent of whom have no high school diploma, and 40 percent of whom have been court-involved. A few programs have become YouthBuild charter schools, which can access state-level public education funding and thus grow to as many as 200 students.

I asked James, Lashon, and Anthony to describe themselves prior to YouthBuild. Their words spilled out: "Impotent... apathetic... lost... full of hatred... judged as inadequate or bad... a life full of drugs and crime... a life on a downward spiral... mom on drugs... dad in jail... sometimes no food or electricity... headed for the grave." Involved in dealing drugs and a part of a gang, James saw one brother die at the hands of a gang and another wind up in jail. Yet with careers opening up and each communicating a palpable almost tangible sense of optimism, the three young men seemed to convey disbelief that these words once described them.

Considering that the population entering YouthBuild has few skills, broken pasts, grim futures, rock bottom self-confidence, and no hope, YouthBuild can point to success rates that astound. Over the years, 17 studies conducted by well-known researchers, such as Professors Ron Ferguson at Harvard, Andrew Hahn at Brandeis, Mark Cohen at Vanderbuilt, and Andrew Wygand from Social Policy Research Associates, have reported excellent results and explained the principles behind them. Manpower Demonstration Research Corporation (MDRC) has recently reported on the process by which YouthBuild programs funded by the U.S. Department of Labor achieve success through annual rigorous data collection processes. YouthBuild USA reports a 71 percent graduation rate, with 77 percent of enrollees earning a high school diploma, GED, and/or industry-recognized credentials, and 61 percent of enrollees placed in college or jobs. The recidivism after one year is a very low 10 percent, compared with a 25 percent national average, a rate continuing to fall well under national recidivism rates after three years (28 percent compared with 67 percent). The students succeed and the community benefits: 10,000 students build 1,000 units of affordable housing each year. Because most YouthBuild graduates are working or in school, the government and taxpayer benefit, because fewer YouthBuild participants get into trouble or become enmeshed in a government "system" such as probation, mental health or corrections. Thus the return on investment is high: according to one study by Professor Mark Cohen, a minimum of $8.70 for every dollar spent on every student.

Those impressive numbers translate into changed lives. James said, "I'm in a good place now. I see me and my brothers with potential now. We are destined to do great things. YouthBuild saw our potential. They showed us caring adults that looked like us, people that talked to us as equals, people who didn't blame us, people who were there consistently." Lashon noted with a smile that it was "not all people that looked like us". Looking at Dorothy, his face glowing with admiration, he said, "When we first met, this old white lady took notes on what I said. Took notes! She felt I had something of worth to say. This white lady really listens. I couldn't believe it. I'm here for whatever she needs. I'm here for her always." "Old?" protested Dorothy with a grin. James commented that he'd gone back to his family in Columbus, OH, to motivate them, to show them a positive role model. "I have a mission for others. They talk now about wanting 'to grow up like James.' They never had a role model before."

Anthony spoke about how he left his city of origin in Tennessee, because he was mired in street life, and came to Boston because he had heard of the YouthBuild program there. Now he is a proud member of the brick layers' union, safe in a productive lifestyle, far from the death and destruction he had expected back home.

The Secret Sauce

How does YouthBuild do it? Some elements are clear and traditional. But it is important to understand YouthBuild's secret sauce. Skill development? Yes, but only in part. Examining the core building blocks provide some clues:

- Supervised Training—pre-apprentice training leading to industry-recognized certification in construction;
- Leadership—including training in decision-making, public speaking, civic engagement, and community service;
- Education—including academic skills, cultural history, GED/Diploma preparation, and bridge to college;
- Service—including building housing for homeless neighbors in need;
- Counseling—individual and peer;

- Resources for Graduates—including college and job placement, mentoring, career counseling, and career supports.

In addition, YouthBuild has expanded its construction track to additional career paths including health care, technology and customer service.

YouthBuild USA cites 11 management factors for success, among them, absolute agency commitment, a full-time director, clear lines of accountability, men of color on staff, and youth involvement in decision making.

This package, the core elements and the delivery structure convey a great deal about the essential elements of YouthBuild, but not all.

To this writer, it's in the sauce that drenches YouthBuild's main menu. YouthBuild USA calls them core values: Love, work, respect, responsibility, community and knowledge, values that appear in YouthBuild's descriptive material. Woven into operations, these values are active, not aspirational, not window-dressing. YouthBuild participants recite a pledge daily, a pledge each YouthBuild site creates on its own. Although pledges differ, each pledge references these values, which help to create a "culture," not a program, rather an ethos, a norm.

"Love? How can you possibly build 'love' into a program?" I asked Dorothy and the three guys. Lashon answered first. "This is not a program," he said vehemently. "Get this: first day I walked in here I got a hug. Whoa, where am I, in a church? It's hard to put your finger on, but you can see it. You can feel it. And the alumni come back to help, too. It's a big community. And we're part of the decision-making, too."

Dorothy immediately seized on Lashon's "decision-making" comment. "We've flipped the power dynamics here. This helps to shape the YouthBuild program. Four YouthBuild graduates sit on our board of directors. Every local program is expected to have a policy council of students with whom the program director meets once a week to ask for their input on the key issues facing the program, to get a real sense of what's happening, where support is needed and what we need to change. That shows our respect for them and our love. We're doing this together."

Anthony jumped in on the "love" question. "It's the way they teach, man. They take the time to know you. Not like the other teachers I had. I didn't get fractions for years. The teacher here taught me fractions in one-half hour because she took the time to know how I learned. She knows how to play your music. The staff doesn't let you go. They go way above and beyond. If you stumble, and we all do, they'll be knocking at your door, getting you up. Wherever I am, hospital or school, they're there. And they never give up! They really want the program to be the best for us. They're not worried about statistics."

Dorothy remarked that YouthBuild USA deliberately encourages all local staff to surprise the young people with how much they care, to go beyond what the young people would expect, to build their trust. In fact, she said, staff are eager to go outside the limits other institutions might put on their roles, where "creating boundaries" has often been encouraged rather than showing commitment.

James remarked that YouthBuild is a place where you can be vulnerable. "They know all your stuff, and they still accept me. Man, you can just feel it. My blood just pumps." It is difficult to overestimate the profound importance—and rarity—of James' observation. Most YouthBuild youth emerge from highly unstable, even dangerous contexts where showing vulnerability can lead to trouble, even death.

Such a remarkable confession of vulnerability means that YouthBuild has created a safe place, a healthy caring community, embedded in some of the most hard-pressed and least safe communities in America. "Safety and constant encouragement and support liberate the latent talent that is otherwise invisible or suppressed," asserts Dorothy. "Young people growing up in poverty," she continues, "often use all of their talents just to survive or to combat the negative conditions surrounding them."

Lashon chimed in: "I couldn't believe my counselor spoke with me for so long. He kept asking me my opinion. Nobody has ever asked me my opinion."

But how do you operationalize a principle like "respect?" I questioned. "Well, they ask us to be part of the decisions," offered Lashon. "And they hold us to a high standard. They expect us to be better. Nobody has expected us to be better. They stress being mentally tough—be on time, be ready, produce, try hard."

James offered that young people have no victories to which they can point or someone who can let them know that the little things they're doing are really big. To attend his YouthBuild program in Columbus, OH, James had to leave the house at 4:30 am, walk for one hour to catch the 5:30 bus, which he rode for another hour. "Best thing was, they celebrated me just getting there. I always had a hard time finishing things. Now I stay until I'm finished. That's a really good feeling because I never had that feeling before."

Not only has YouthBuild changed lives, but it has changed and is now embedded in federal policy. YouthBuild is authorized in the Workforce Investment Opportunity Act, which is administered by the Department of Labor. Annual appropriations from Congress to the Department of Labor total about $80 million to support the Department's annual competition for community-based non-profits or public entities to apply for grants of $1.1 million for two years of funding and one year of follow up. While only a handful of initiatives can point to such success, and while precious few initiatives have gained such ringing and manifest federal endorsement and support, federal funds are, according to Dorothy, "insufficient. Not only is every program serving only a fraction of the young people who apply and DOL only funding a small fraction of the communities who apply for federal YouthBuild funds, but the federal grants do not even cover all the costs of YouthBuild programs that are funded." She notes with passion that there are at least 2.3 million low-income 16-24 years olds in the U.S. who are not in education, employment, or training. Making things even more difficult: Labor requires a 25 percent non-federal match.

Funds from business and philanthropic sources help. Some cities and states, among them Minnesota, Massachusetts and New York City, fund their local YouthBuild programs directly, which creates a truly important foundation for sustainability. Some programs tap into other federal funds such as Community Development Block Grants, city or state public education monies, or the Corporation for National and Community Service funds.

Dorothy had the final word on that rainy November day, taking the notion of "program" to another level altogether. "People just have to understand that this is not simply a skill development program. YouthBuild releases the energy and talent of young people who didn't feel they had anything to offer anybody. It lets them know they can be contributors, leaders, that they can play an important part in rebuilding their communities and changing society to increase opportunity and decrease poverty, increase love, healthy communities, and responsibility for all. It breaks the cycle of poverty and hopelessness. Breaks it. This is not a program: it's a way of life."

RESOURCES

- YouthBuild (http://www.YouthBuild.org): To ensure fidelity to the philosophy, culture and components of the model, YouthBuild USA works with the Department of Labor as a training/technical assistant provider for its grantees.
  (http://www.doleta.gov/youth_services/youthbuild.cfm)
- Center for Law and Social Policy (CLASP) (http://www.clasp.org/)

- Heartland Alliance National Initiatives
- (http://www.heartlandalliance.org/)
- Institute for Educational Leadership—Center for Workforce Development (http://www.ncwd-youth.info/node/167)
- Jobs for the Future (JFF) (http://www.jff.org/)
- MDRC (http://www.mdrc.org/)
- NLC YEF Institute (http://www.nlc.org/find-city-solutions/ institute-for-youth-education-and-families)
- National Youth Employment Coalition (NYEC) (https://www.nyec.org/)

OTHER AGENCIES SERVING YOUTH:

- Afterschool Alliance (http://www.afterschoolalliance.org) is dedicated to raising awareness of the importance of after school programs.
- School Dropout Prevention Programs, U.S. Department of Education (http://www2.ed.gov/programs/dropout/index.html) supports effective dropout prevention and reentry programs in high schools with annual drop-out rates exceeding their state average drop-out rate.
- National Dropout Prevention Center (http://dropoutprevention.org/modelprograms) provides listings of model dropout prevention programs..
- Big Brothers Big Sisters of America (http://www.bbbsa.org) makes meaningful monitored matches between adult volunteers and children ages 6 through 18 in communities across America.
- Boys and Girls Clubs of America (http://bgca.org/pages/index.aspx) works with young people, especially those in greatest need to reach their full potential.

- YMCA (http://www.ymca.net) strengthens communities by helping kids and families in need reach their full potential.
- YWCA (http://www.ywca.org), through advocacy and local programming, creates real change for women, families and communities.
- Restorative Justice (http://restorativejustice.org) develops and promotes restorative justice in the criminal justice systems around the world.
- National Institute of Justice (http://www.nij.gov/topics/courts/restorative-justice/pages/welcome.aspx) gives full descriptions and policy implications of, and research base for restorative justice programs.
- Reclaiming Youth International/Starr Commonwealth (https://www.starr.org/training/youth) Dedicated to the development of programs and strategies to serve children and youth who are in conflict in families, schools and communities.

POLICY WALKING

CHAPTER 7

Community Renewal:

Changing Norms & Building Resilient Communities

"When we first got here, the kids were talking about drive-by shootings, gangs and drugs. And now we've gone from fear to quiet. Now we feel safe enough to have a baby here."

— Josh Harville, Shreveport Resident

POLICY

Communities exhibiting high social cohesion and robust civic participation can point to lower rates of crime. Conversely, civic disconnection and neighborhood neglect leads to suspicion if not fear, high crime and low intra-neighborhood support and caring. Can collapsing, mistrusting neighborhoods change? Community Renewal International (CRI) claims they can because they've helped to build them

I wasn't sure I believed it. Picture a rough neighborhood: shabby, small houses; a general store with a faded sign now overgrown with weeds; few people in the streets. But then, voila, a large, brilliantly painted house framed by a lush lawn, welcoming with a wrap-around porch. Surreal. Almost Disney-esque. But there it is. The neighborhood loves it. The kids flock to it. I've seen it first-hand, walked the streets, talked to youth and residents who, until now, had only wanted to move out. Can community norms really change? CRI is proving that they can.

WALKING

In 1994, the city of Shreveport, LA, was hit by Hurricane Mack McCarter, a storm neither named nor seen by the U.S. Weather Service.

McCarter, who swept in from Texas to return to the city in which he grew up, was hell (or heaven) bent on sweeping away old stereotypes, changing conventional wisdom about how to reclaim frightened, crime-ridden communities and ready to uproot social norms that most felt could not be changed.

McCarter's mission transcends neighborhood transformation. He attempts through CRI, a non-profit he founded in 1994, to provide the solution to the problem of societal decay, asserting that the answer lies in a simple rule of life: give positive, committed and intentional attention to a human relationship, and it will grow stronger, and it will spread.

I've done street work, but I'm also a policy guy. I press Mack, highly skeptical of his thesis, telling him that this sounds, well, pretty soft. Mack quickly responds by citing Lewis Mumford, a sociologist and historian, who observed, "the chief enigma of history is found in the question, 'Why do we keep collapsing the societies we construct?'" Mack believes passionately "that societies continue to collapse because we neglect the very foundation upon which those societies stand." He asserts that the foundation is composed of people connected together in many ways—a foundation of human relationships. When relationships are ignored or taken for granted, Mack contends, they diminish. "Criminal activity, domestic violence, child neglect, substance abuse, high school dropout rates and other problems are all symptoms of a society with a fundamental lack of caring relationships," he says vehemently. Disintegrating relationships bring about collapse on a massive scale.

CRI's model addresses five essential family protective factors identified by the research community:

- Parental resilience
- Social connections
- Knowledge of parenting and child development
- Concrete support in times of need
- Children's social and emotional development

CRI's mission—to bring "together caring partners to make our world a home where every single person is safe and loved" stems directly from its understanding of these protective factors. CRI aims to systematically initiate, grow and sustain safe and loving communities that produce measurable results. Grounded in the conviction that "love wins out in the end," CRI focuses on making neighborhoods and communities safer and healthier by the creation of a rich tapestry of caring, sustained relationships.

The model rests on three building blocks, which begin in core neighborhoods and then fan out to the entire city: Friendship Houses, Haven Houses and the "The Renewal Team" that supports thousands of "We Care" team members.

Friendship Houses built in mistrusting, high-crime neighborhoods feature a large community room for tutoring, music and art, computer use, mentoring and more. A CRI Friendship House is a safe haven in the community, a caring place where children and teens receive love and support they need to become responsible, successful adults who give back to the community. Volunteers and key partners—from The Fuller Center for Housing to local banks and churches (Mack's Active Partners' List runs six pages—about 250 names in all)–build these large houses with the community as an active partner. CRI cautions those who would initiate programs in troubled communities, must ensure support and ownership by the local community, if so programs results will be greatly enhanced. Trained staff and their families live in these homes, modeling family, and rebuilding the infrastructure of the area by working with the children, youth and adults in the neighborhood, using the rooms both as classrooms, and as community centers. CRI has set a goal of building and staffing 60 Friendship Houses.

Hurricane McCarter aimed first at families living in hard-pressed neighborhoods. He didn't stop there. In efforts to inculcate caring as a citywide norm, he next created "Haven Houses." More than 1,350 Haven House block leaders (with attractive Haven House signs on their front lawns) are trained to restore the relational foundations on the blocks where they live. Pledged to "remake our city by making friends on our block," Haven House volunteers do everything from welcoming new neighbors, to providing helpful information on any number of issues—libraries, sports opportunities, child care, where to vote, and the time and place of the next block party.

The third building block—the "Renewal Team" that supports the "We Care members"—is the most expansive and visible. You're standing in the supermarket checkout line somewhere in Shreveport. The person in front of you sports a "We Care" button. The line is long, so you engage in conversation, asking what the button means and where to get one. The answer: You apply for it, and get your button only after you've filled out a card on which you pledge to "keep caring" or to "care" for someone else (could be tutoring a youngster or weekly calls to your uncle who has cancer). 50,000 (yes, fifty thousand) Shreveporters have earned their "We Care" buttons.

Relationships do not necessarily feed and clothe. Elizabeth Beauvais, CRI's former director of strategic growth, asserts that once the "relational foundation," a system of intentional and caring relationships that undergirds a community, is in place, then "programs that address important needs, such as education, safety and work, can take firm hold and thrive."

Namby-pamby? Mushy? A strategy based on enhancing relationships that can produce results? Yes. Anchored solidly in the works of Mumford, author Jane Jacobs (who penned *The Death and Life of Great American Cities*), historian Arnold Toynbee, and the theologian Elton Trueblood, CRI can show results via statistics and personal testimony:

- In target neighborhoods, a 45% drop in major crime.
- "We're seeing a real facelift. There are law-abiding citizens here now. I hardly ever get calls anymore," says the Police Department's Cpl. Mike Dunn.
- "This is like a double ray of sunshine. Now I can walk to the bus on streets I would not walk on before," said Reola Cormbe, a resident.

Mack can wax eloquent about Mumford, Jacobs and Toynbee, but, to me, the aggregation of small vignettes I heard from local citizens are the most eloquent, vignettes that might not make it into a research canon, but are, nonetheless, testimonies to stunning changes in a neighborhood's ethos: "Pizza being delivered here for the first time in years," or "taxis never dared to come here, and now they do," and comments about being able to get to school safely or to take the bus with impunity.

Pizza, taxis, busses, safe walking...important? You bet: taken together all speak to what one might label civic measures—dramatic changes in a community's quality of life.

In 2009, CRI conducted a mailed survey with individuals known to We Care team members including active Haven House block leaders and residents and volunteers in the Friendship House target neighborhoods. Among the stunning results:

- They have more hope

- They have a better understanding of how to work with others to get things done
- They make more of a difference in their community
- They have more people in their lives who care
- They have developed additional skills to solve problems and reach their goals
- They have a better understanding of the community
- They feel that they and their friends are more capable of making changes in their community
- They feel that they are more capable of making changes in the city

In short, respondents wanted to make changes, felt confident that they could make changes and collectively they made changes.

- The lives of more than 3,000 children and youth have been transformed
- In 2015 alone, 1,909 volunteers contributed 36,794 volunteer hours
- Renewal team memberships in 41 nations and 50 states total 51,600, a number that continues to grow
- There are 1,450 trained Neighborhood Block Leaders in Shreveport alone
- CRI has been replicated completely or in part in:
  - Abilene, TX (www.wecareabilene.org)
  - Minneapolis/St. Paul, MN (www.wecaretwincities.org)
  - Shawnee, OK
  - Washington, DC (http://communityrenewal.us) and (www.givingbacktoamerica.us)
  - Cameroon, Africa, in Doumbuo, and the Institute for Philanthropy and Community Renewal in Yaounde
  - Texas Christian University, Ft. Worth, TX

- Since its inception in 1994, volunteers have logged more than 500,000 hours for CRI

CRI works with the Terrorism and Disaster Center (TDC) at the University of Oklahoma Health Sciences Center and is a Category II Center of the National Child Traumatic Stress Network (NCTSN), a national network funded by the Substance Abuse Mental Health Services Administration to improve the standard of care for traumatized children and to increase their access to care. The TDC believes that as no natural disaster can be stopped and as some terror attacks will succeed, resilient communities that can bounce back after disasters must be "grown." The TDC reports being greatly influenced by the CRI model.

At root, CRI is fully committed to rigorously seeking to know whether people are better, the city is better based on deeper relationships of caring. Future evaluations will focus on educational attainment, poverty levels, incidence of reported crime, use of public spaces, and level of community engagement.

Quality of life and crime rates dependent in part on caring? Really? CRI may well be onto something. Dr. Felton Earls, Professor of Human Behavior and Development Emeritus at Harvard's T.H. Chan School of Public Health, argues that the most important influence on a neighborhood's crime rate is the neighbors' willingness to act, when needed, for one another's benefit, and particularly for the benefit of one another's children (Hurley, Dan. "On Crime as Science – A Neighbor at a Time", January 6, 2004. Rutgers.edu). His social science language calls it "collective efficacy." A profoundly simply concept lies under the polysyllabic language: neighbors who care about each other, care about each other's children, care about the neighborhood make a difference in crime rates and the quality of neighborhood life (ibid.).

Earls' revolutionary findings were triggered by his discovery of anomalies – pockets of low crime in Chicago's high crime areas. His pioneering work, the Chicago Neighborhood Study, garnered support from the National Institute of Justice (NIJ), the MacArthur Foundation and others. Jeremy Travis who directed the NIJ from 1994 to 2000 said of Earls' work, "I think it will shape policy for the next generation." Francis Cullen, past president of the American Society of Criminology concurred: "It is perhaps the most important research undertaking ever embarked upon in the study of criminal behavior" (ibid.).

As Mack asserts, an assertion backed by research, the urban poor's ability to survive and thrive, is highly dependent on neighborhood social structures.

Along with nine Nobel laureates, Bill Gates, Desmond Tutu and a diverse array of political, humanitarian and economic leaders from around the globe, McCarter, in 2008 and 2009, participated in former President Bill Clinton's annual summit of the Clinton Global Initiative. Former President Jimmy Carter honored the work with his keynote speech at CRI's 20th Anniversary Celebration on October 30, 2014.

The late Millard Fuller, founder of Habitat for Humanity, said of CRI, "You have the premier community renewal building model in the nation. I've never seen a more exciting opportunity than what I see here in Shreveport."

Mack's vision is universal in scope. He fervently tells me that "If we coordinate our caring in a systematic way, then the power of that caring can be so concentrated that it can transform our cities and sustain generational betterment..."

His vision, grand in scope, comes alive when lodged in one person's heart. Listen to Joseph, a Friendship House graduate. "It has been a blessing to be in an environment where people actually love you, knowing the broken home that I come from. The years I have been here have made me a leader."

RESOURCES

- Community Renewal International (http://www.communityrenewal.us)
- Communities that Care (http://www.communitiesthatcare.net) is a proven community change process for reducing youth violence through tested and effective programs.
- Hurley, Dan, "On Crime as Science – A Neighbor at a Time" (http://crab.rutgers.edu/~goertzel/CollectiveEfficacyEarls.html)

CHAPTER 8

Faith in Action

"The faith community's work starts not with program or policy, but with the forging of relationships with people living in the neighborhood."

When preparing my remarks for the Episcopal Divinity School's Alumni Reunion in the spring of 2015, the two core aspects of the faith community's work—the personal/relational and the prophetic—dredged up a 50-year-old memory. Somehow the memory adhered. Dr. Martin Luther King Jr.'s public ministry had affected divinity schools across the nation. It had affected me. I marched. In point of fact, I attended divinity school because of King. In a burst of adolescent indignation following the news of beatings, hosings, and, yes, the murders of civil rights workers in the south, I burst into the dean's office demanding that he empty the school. "People are dying in the streets," I recall saying. "The bishop's wife has been jailed. And you're still here? Why isn't the faculty in the streets? Why is this school still open?" Dean Coburn looked at me with his renowned calmness, understanding and implicit forgiveness of my self-righteousness and said, "We're keeping the Ark of the Covenant alive here. Keeping the school and the church open restores, gives you the courage to go out into the streets. We are here to sustain you as you witness publicly. Without this you won't be reminded why you're doing what you're doing."

Most faith communities subscribe to distinct but complementary traditions: virtuous living, a relationship with God, righteousness, and personal healing ministries. The other, equally strong, is the call of the prophets to feed the hungry, clothe the naked, visit those in prison, and speak out against inequities—in short, social justice. It is not just prayer and the need for personal forgiveness that drives a member of the faith community, but also the need for action. In response to neighborhood crime and violence, faith communities throughout the nation, especially those located in crime-ridden, mistrusting communities, have waded into and sometimes led efforts to stop violence and build "the beloved community." They have healed and marched, prayed and protested, taught and testified.

POLICY

Many neighborhood violence-prevention initiatives address some of the most volatile and dangerous situations in some of the most turbulent and mistrusting areas of their respective cities. Violence interrupters mediate disputes, stand between hostile individuals or groups, and—often from hospital bedsides—attempt to head off retaliation. Case managers try to link victims and victimizers to school, to job opportunities, and to positive adults, and often work to help stabilize families. Program leaders form essential partnerships with law enforcement, probation officers, child welfare, schools, and local service organizations. Whether named community norm change, community mobilization, or community health, each neighborhood initiative, in addition to working with people, aims to improve the community context in which youth who are at the greatest risk survive. And many, if not most, of the neighborhood initiatives rely on the faith community or people grounded in faith to do or support this work.

Street work, program administration, and community norms: it is a tall order, and uncertainty abounds. A young person from a rough neighborhood, enrolled in a GED program or as an apprentice, might be shot and killed on the way home, while a tough teen returning from a detention center might celebrate receiving his or her community college degree.

Neighborhood work plays out in zip codes characterized by high poverty, manifest police/community mistrust, domestic violence and child abuse, low school or job connection, and low expectations. Loss and hope are constant companions. Yet, such efforts persist, changing lives and even entire neighborhoods. In the face of this uncertainty, one must have faith that change is possible – and one must have the faith community to help put that faith into action. Other than local families themselves, no entity other than the faith community knows the neighborhood as well.

For this to work well, allies—especially from the faith community—are needed. Faith-based entities, for the most part, are not seen as outside service providers or responders. They are in the community, know the community, and know intimately what children, youth, and families face as residents. All too often they deal directly with grief and trauma. Many of those sitting in church pews have witnessed violence, some have daughters and sons in jail, and some have lost loved ones. The faith community's work starts not with program or policy, but with the forging of relationships with people living in the neighborhood.

"They know the streets," said Boston Police Commissioner William Evans about the faith-based community. "They know the gangs. They know the kids."

Peter Kim, program manager for Oakland, California's Community-based Violence Prevention Program intends to forge more robust relationships with the faith community—a more "direct service–oriented" approach. Kim views houses of worship as resources for "mentorship, food and shelter, employment opportunities, and trauma-informed healing."

But the role of the faith community can be that and so much more. Clergy and congregations have mentored, tutored, and fed and clothed the hungry. They have also marched, served on local governing boards, and testified before city councils and state legislatures. The relational and the prophetic are intimately linked, especially for the African American community, where the church has served both as a place of restoration and as a place where plans to address social justice issues, such as voting rights and fair housing, are forged.

Faith-based entities providing necessary social services can trigger controversy – raising the issue of separation of church and state. Three types of services provided by the faith community exist: faith-filled, faith-linked, and faith-based. "Faith-filled" programs have typically rejected public funding because they mandate religious participation as a condition of receiving services. America has been utilizing the services of "faith-linked" organizations since the 19th century. When I served as Commissioner of Youth Services in Massachusetts, some of the most effective and valued contractors were Catholic Charities, Jewish Family and Children's Services, and Christian Children's Home. Many Head Start programs are located in churches. In these, services are not intertwined with faith. This leaves the middle ground, "faith-based" programs. Here faith is neither a prerequisite nor a mandatory part of the program, but faith is nearby, within reach, readily accessible. The Valley, which once operated in space provided by the Cathedral of St. John the Divine in New York City, dealt with some of Harlem's toughest kids. The program, supported by foundation and public funds, included intensive mentoring, GED work, job training and a weekly "Grace Circle." The Grace Circle was not required, but its former director, John Bess, said it's "so personal and so supportive. The kids never missed it."

We should be clear. Faith entities must meet the same rules as other non-profits. Their work must not be taken on faith, but on results. Are at-risk kids staying in school, addicts off drugs, parolees out of prison? Measureable results are necessary, even in the face of immeasurable challenges. The work is tough. Each must ask him or herself: would I be there for the troubled and the troubling—the juvenile returning from prison, the violently angry adult? Can I endure the anger and the pain? Can I live my faith but not compel others to do so? There are few who can answer "yes." For those who can.let them keep their faith as they go about the public good.

WALKING

Abraham Heschel, author of *Moral Grandeur and Spiritual Audacity* and one of the 20th century's most brilliant theologians, felt politics and theology were inextricably linked. After the civil rights march in Selma, AL, he said, "I felt my legs were praying." There are many great examples of those who have linked arms with faith leaders and organizations as they walk their policies forward.

For Amy Ellenbogen, director of the Crown Heights Mediation Center in New York City, the faith community serves as an essential partner. Manifesting her full commitment to involve faith leaders, Ellenbogen has hired a "clergy consultant"—a liaison to the faith community who hosts breakfasts and education sessions on topics such as the link between domestic and gun violence and trauma-informed services. The liaison pays particular attention to the pain clergy witness on a daily basis, and *their* need for healing. Ellenbogen relies on the clergy as a critical and trusted communication vehicle. She can quickly disseminate information about police or city concerns through the clergy network, which, in turn, reaches those most affected. Together with the faith community, Ellenbogen has developed a clear protocol in response to a shooting. That protocol combines a healing/grief strategy with the ongoing development of a "community norm," where violence is viewed as unacceptable, abnormal.

Boston has redoubled its anti-violence efforts, partnering with the faith community since the early 1990s. Jason Whyte, program manager for the Boston Police Department, cites numerous examples of faith-based violence prevention work. The faith community helps establish relationships with at-risk kids. Churches in the Black Ministerial Alliance in Mattapan (under contract with Action for

Boston Community Development) serve as sites for the arts, recreation, and employment. Police team up with kids to run Youth Café Friday Nights, which improves youth–police dialogue and works to keep young people safe. The iconic Operation Night Light connects faith leaders with police and/or probation officers to visit the homes of known offenders. These visits show offenders that the community cares and is willing to assist, but that it will not tolerate future misbehavior.

"We cannot do our work without the faith community," proclaims Paul Callanan, director of the Gang Reduction Initiative of Denver. His work with faith leaders occurs in three areas: the streets, relational ministries, and responses to grief and loss; programs, such as taking kids on excursions to the mountains, hosting "Say No to Violence" basketball tournaments, prayer walks in volatile neighborhoods; and finally, the structural, the clergy as part of his governing body. Next up for Callanan: the church as a "safe haven after [a] shooting." "Right now," he explains, "those who have been victimized by a shooting must go all over the city to get help from different sources." Callanan envisions gathering those services (Red Cross aid, trauma treatment, food, etc.) in one central, convenient, and trusted place.

Although a prosecutor, Charles "Joe" Hynes, District Attorney, Kings County, Brooklyn, New York, has done all in his power to keep young offenders from penetrating further into the criminal justice system. One of the many programs launched by Joe, Youth and Congregations in Partnership (YCP) aims to prevent further criminal activity and self-destructive behaviors by providing mentoring and comprehensive services for young offenders. Individuals recruited from faith institutions—Christian, Jewish and Muslim—are trained to serve as mentors for participating youth. His office reports that YCP youth recidivate less than youth not enrolled in the program.

In the late 1990s, Boston reported the steepest decline in youth violence in the nation – no teen homicides in two years. Dubbed the "Boston Miracle," it was catalyzed by a gunfight between rival gangs in a church during a funeral service following which local ministers joined forces to form the "10-Point Coalition." They soon launched "Ceasefire" where ministers served as mediators between the police, community, and gang members. Ministers offer support and services in exchange for a gang member's pledge to stop the violence. If violent activity resumes, the community along with ministers, fully support the police in bringing the youth to justice. The Reverend Jeffrey Brown, who played and continues to play a key role in Boston and throughout the nation, spurns the "Miracle" label. "It wasn't a miracle," he asserts. "It was the result of the hard work of leaders, from traditionally-conflicting constituencies, and many of them unsung, coming together to check their egos at the door, and valuing the collective strength of our efforts as more than what we could do individually. We stopped looking at gang youth as the-problem-to-be-solved, and started seeing them as partners and co-laborers in the effort to seek peace in our city." (Note: Involving youth is explored more fully in Chapter 4, "Youth as Resources.")

Throughout the nation's history, the faith community has played a central and catalytic role in the nation's most seismic changes: abolition of slavery, women's right to vote and the Civil Rights Movement, led by the Rev. Dr. Martin Luther King Jr. The faith community is again called into the breach, standing between a gap of mistrust yawning between the police and the community, one of the most salient and contentious policy issues of today. The faith community has placed itself in the middle of efforts to reconcile, to heal, not wound, include, not exclude. In this the work begins with the personal, not institutional and it includes a commitment to honesty and transparency, constant communication, a willingness to tackle the most sensitive issues, and a readiness to be accountable.

Scott Larson, pastor and director of Straight Ahead Ministries in Massachusetts, bases his work on faith when dealing with toughest youth offenders. Working locally and internationally, Straight Ahead begins its work in lock up through reentry "providing structure and support through each step of an individual's journey of faith." Companion programs include gang reconciliation, a job-readiness training program through Straight2Work, and an international ministry, now in Haiti, the Ukraine and India, which aims "to create an international movement whereby every youth who is locked up has the opportunity to hear and respond to the gospel and grow into all God has created them to be" (www.straightahead.org). Although openly faith-filled, Straight Ahead Ministries receives both private and public funding, much of it from the state's Department of Youth Services—this because of its success with the most hard-core young offenders.

Tony Ortiz, pastor and former gang member, founded California Youth Outreach (CYO) in San Quentin, and soon moved to the street where it concentrated its activities on prevention. CYO "reaches out to gang-impacted youth, their families and communities by means of educational services, intervention programs and resource opportunities that support a positive and healthy lifestyle" (www.cyoutreach.org). Although somewhat less manifestly faith-filled than Straight Ahead, Tony, winner of The California Wellness Foundation's Peace Prize, says, "I could not do this work without my faith. Impossible. Fear would cripple me. Uncertainty would cripple me. Perfect love casts out all fear. All fear. I know no fear. I know perfect love." Although a man of faith, Tony didn't really want to be ordained, but the California authorities didn't want the old troublemaker back in their jails. Ordination was his only route in. "I asked my pastor how to get ordained," Tony told me. "I really didn't care about it. I just wanted a way to get in to see those kids." (Larson and Ortiz are also featured in my earlier book *Hope Matters*, 2011, Bartleby Press.)

In Long Beach, CA, Pastor Gregory Sanders, President of the Long Beach Ministerial Alliance, shares thoughts with Police Academy students, advises on hiring and helps the Police Department identify those areas in the city that "are hurting most," those "experiencing trauma," those on the edge of trouble. And he works closely with the police department in crisis situations. Sanders speaks frequently of "transparency." By this he means full disclosure, a willingness to identify mistakes, "tell it like it is," while working toward solutions. Sanders is trusted and might be called an honest broker. Theologically framed, he is a reconciler.

Pastor Danny Sanchez, founder of The City Peace Project, winner of President Obama's Champion of Change Award in 2012 and who was involved in the gang lifestyle, echoed the reconciliation theme, describing its manifestation in three separate programs. Individuals in several parishes throughout the city have, through Adopt a Cop, signed up to pray for individual law enforcement officers. They connect through a website. Officers can be people of faith, "or of little faith or no faith," says Sanchez. "The important thing is that the officers know they're loved and appreciated."

Pastor Sanchez also created the City Chaplaincy Program. Sanchez, the lead chaplain, and his team work with police and the other community and faith-based organizations to go "under the tape" into the trauma and messiness of families torn apart by homicide. "Services" provided range from prayer and help with rent, food, and funeral expenses to links to counseling and on-going support for the wide-ranging needs of each remaining family member. Through the "Trauma to Triumph" program at Santa Clara County Valley Medical Hospital, Sanchez's faith-based team, while providing basic services for victimized families, attempts to stop retaliation.

Sanchez also takes kids at risk of gang involvement (as well as some already in gangs) to police department headquarters where they meet with police Captain Anthony Mata. When he first proposed it to them, the youth recoiled in horror: "We don't want to go to jail." He reassured them that his purpose had little to do with the law. "It has to do with our youth getting to know the officers as people." Sanchez describes how "the Captain opens up, tells his story, what he was like as a kid." Then the youth get to explore different areas of the department and sit in the police cars. The Captain provides tips on how to react if approached by an officer and how and where to complain if they feel unjustly treated. Sanchez reports that youth could not believe that the officers, swathed in uniforms, wearing guns were "real people."

In Oxnard, CA, women connected to local churches have a simple, but profound, mission: be with and show affection for third graders, many of whom come from fragmented families with little consistency. Called "Grandmother Hugs," the program is just that. Volunteers hug the children. Said one women, "It's so wonderful and so sad. Sad because the line is long for the hugs they're not getting at home. And wonderful because of the smiles we put on their faces. They wait for us every week."

RESOURCES

- Winship, Christopher and Berrien, Jenny, *Boston Cops and Black Churches*, Public Interest, 1999
- Winship, Christopher and Braga, Anthony, *Creating an Effective Partnership to Prevent Youth Violence: Lessons Learned from Boston in the 1990s*, Rappaport Institute Policy Brief, 2005
- My City at Peace (http://www.mycityatpeace.com) is based on the work of Rev. Jeffrey Brown; this unique community-based solution builds alliances between traditionally conflicting constituencies to find peace and end violence in communities. My City at Peace equips and trains clergy with the skills to walk the streets of the most violent neighborhoods and engage with youth at the heart of violence. Rev. Brown is the speaker of a popular TED Talk entitled "How We Cut Youth Violence in Boston by 79%." (https://youtu.be/yeVz0rtXCmw)
- *Faith and Communities in Action: A Resource Guide for Increasing Partnership Opportunities to Prevent Crime and Violence*, Bureau of Justice Assistance, Office of Justice Programs, U.S. Department of Justice (http://ojp.gov/fbnp/pdfs/communityaction.pdf)
- Calhoun, Jack, *Hope Matters*, Bartleby Press, 2011 (http://www.HopeMatters.org)
- The City Peace Project (http://www.thecitypeaceproject.org)
- Straight Ahead Ministries (http://www.straightahead.org)
- California Youth Outreach (http://www.cyoutreach.org)

POLICY WALKING

CHAPTER 9

Community Trust and The "New" Policing

"Knowing the community, caring for the community,
building trust and protecting the community come first.
Enforcement, if necessary, last."

POLICY

The term "law enforcement" has, unfortunately skewed what police do or should be doing. Yes, police enforce, but to enforce well, they've got to know their community, and, to know the community, they've got to establish trust. The best departments are seen first as protectors, those who know their community intimately, the parks, the schools, the hot spots, the people, and the community's trusted institutions. They are viewed as an integral part of the community, not an external force summoned in times of emergency. When enforcement is needed, they will enforce. But that's not where they should start.

Police practice and the philosophy of policing is under examination across the nation. Police shootings of apparently defenseless citizens in several cities across America in 2015 triggered citizen outrage and in some cases, riots—cars overturned and burned, local businesses, trashed. The unrest threw into stark relief questions about who the police were policing, how they were policing and the nature of policing itself. Were the police "your friend," "your police," or were they an occupying force, "their police." Were the police "warriors" ready to enforce or "protectors" of their communities? Whiter and wealthier neighborhoods give higher marks to the police than Blacks and Latinos. The higher the level of violent crime in the community, the lower the ratings for the police.

Morale is low on both sides. Many citizens in certain communities are scared and angry. Police are too, for officers have been shot and killed. Given a nation awash in guns, police feel that the community doesn't realize or appreciate the fact that even a routine traffic stop can turn into a gunfight. Is the driver actually reaching in the glove compartment for his registration or a gun? Many citizens maintain that the police don't know them, don't even try to know them and are more an outside force than an integral part of a network of community protection, a network of mutual trust, in essence, together for the co-production of safety.

In response to citizen outcries and voices in the law enforcement community calling for reform, President Obama formed the Task Force on 21st Century Policing, chaired by Ron Davis, head of the Community Oriented Policing Services Office and a former Chief of Police in East Palo Alto, California. Its job? Provide recommendations to the President on how policing practices can promote effective crime reductions while building public trust and examine, among other issues, how to foster strong, collaborative relationships between law enforcement and the communities they protect.

Task Force recommendations cluster in six areas: changing the culture of policing from warriors to guardians, embracing community policing, ensuring fair and impartial policing ("procedural justice"), building community capital that grows from positive interaction, and attending to officer wellness and safety. While tension—including street protests—continues unabated in several cities across America, many cities, tailoring Task Force recommendations to their unique community situations have begun to make positive changes. As noted below, a few cities have been at it for some time.

WALKING

Yet even before the Task Force recommendations were promulgated, there were signs from across the nation that policing had begun to change.

In the Hebbron district of Salinas, CA, two officers, Rich Lopez and Jeffery Lofton were stationed in a youth center. They knew the kids and their families. They got to know the neighborhood by attending community events and meetings, and by knocking on doors introducing themselves, handing out business cards and offering whatever assistance might be needed. Crime in the Hebbron area dropped dramatically. Citizen trust among the locals in this Central California agricultural community, many of whom are undocumented, had soared. One clear sign of citizen trust: more frequent calls for police help—parents asking the police to teach parenting! And they did. "The power of the police is not their power of arrest," asserts Kelly McMillin, Salinas' Police Chief. "An arrest may be necessary, but they can divert a young drug offender to treatment. They can serve as effective convener, helping to mediate neighborhood disputes. They can navigate the bureaucracy, getting potholes repaired, stop signs erected and streetlights replaced. Thus, if an arrest is made, or an officer involved shooting occurs, the community tends to view the police actions as legitimate because they know them and know they care." But this story does not end well. Budget cuts forced Chief McMillin to remove Officers Lopez and Lofton from Hebbron and to cut almost one-third of his overall force. The result? Crime levels are rising again. Despite the sobering resurgence, it, ironically, affirms Chief McMillin's successful Hebbron strategy.

In Camden, NJ, one of American's poorest and most violent cities, crime has dropped to its lowest level in years, "because," asserts Barbara Maronski who directs the city's violence prevention efforts, "the police are going all out to forge positive relationships with the community." The PACER program—Police and Congress Enjoy Reading Program—has officers reading one-on-one with kindergarteners. Via Camden County's Meet and Greet program officers host barbeques and the Blue Knights hold events at parks where officers distribute free T-shirts, while enlisting parents and kids to help keep the parks safe. Police mentor youth through Camden's "Buddy Initiative" and youth pour out to watch Cops vs. Youth basketball games. When on a site visit to Camden in September 2014, one officer said to me, "Policing has never been so rewarding. Not so long ago, I could hardly wait to finish my time and get out of policing. But now I'm going to hate to leave. I love my job."

In the summer of 2015, New York's Mayor de Blasio and his police chief Bill Bratton, unveiled a plan to return to "the cop on the beat." The city's new mantra, "One City: Safe and Fair – Everywhere," follows five Ts: tactics, technology, training, terrorism and trust (*The Economist*, July 11, 2015, p. 32).

In Santa Rosa, CA, police tutor children, coach sports, sit on local non-profit boards, and serve as mentors. The Santa Rosa Police Department's 2014 Annual Report is a model of transparency and accountability, citing all crime statistics including number and type of citizen/police encounters, complaints and the status of complaints. The police annually conduct a comprehensive survey asking citizens what they want, what they feel is needed and how they would evaluate the quality of Santa Rosa's police services.

Many cities have launched police/youth dialogues or forums and several departments have forged close working relationships with the faith community, such as ride-alongs in Sacramento, youth/police dialogues in San Jose, police academy training in Long Beach and Operation Night Light in Boston where police and faith leaders visit the homes of youth most in danger of victimizing others. Examples of the faith community helping to affect police/community trust are noted in Chapter 8, "Faith in Action."

The real question, however, is whether such programs cited above are merely ad hoc: programs sprinkled throughout a police department or whether they represent something deeper, namely a commitment to systemic change in police culture and practice.

Los Angeles' Police Chief Charlie Beck hasn't simply changed policing in the three most violent housing projects in the Watts area of Los Angeles; he has transformed it. The Watts cops sign up for five years. If they stay, they receive two additional stripes. The 35 officers, carefully screened and selected out of a pool of 400 applicants, are rigorously trained with community stakeholders. Community people have a say in the hiring of those who would police them. Community leaders show the new police around, taking them to schools to meet the principals and teachers and to community service and faith leaders. The Community Safety Partnership (CSP) is run by the Urban Peace Institute in Los Angeles. The new policing strategy "imagines a new way of operating for the police where their legitimacy is built on procedural justice, an authentic relationship with community members and sustained commitment to the health and well-being of the community." Promotions are not based solely on traditional enforcement measures, e.g., number of arrests, but on measures such as diverting youthful offenders, helping students travel safely to schools and the nature and extent of contacts with the community. "Yeah, they have to keep the crime down," says Reverend Michael Cummings, a street worker and police/community liaison, "but they got to know the community and so they're worried about us, how we're doing, helping kids have a future." CSP's results are stunning:

- A reduction in violent crime by more than 50%
- Notable decreases in gang membership and activity
- Plummeting homicide rates

I met Reverend Cummings first by phone. He was sitting in his truck outside the school grounds, poised, with the police, to help get the kids home safely from school. His walkie-talkie crackled. What he said in those few minutes, through the crackling connection, the din of children and the hum of traffic noise stunned me. I signed him up on the spot to serve on a panel I was pulling together for the Council on Foundation's annual meeting to be held in San Francisco in April 2015. Cummings presented and received a standing ovation. This very large, gentle man in a long robe held the audience spellbound. Because of police/community riots in Baltimore that week, the Council hastily created a special session on police/community trust. Cummings starred there also. Through his stories, the statistics came alive: "I grew up in Watts. Got jumped into a gang when I was 13: only way I could get to school safely. Otherwise I got beat up every day. We hated the cops. Nobody trusted the cops. If you talked to the cops, you got hurt. Now? I've never seen moms and grandmothers sitting on their front steps waving to cops. They do now in Watts. I've never seen kids running up to cops to get a hug. Happens all the time." Working closely with the police, some of whom he has helped to hire, Michael continues his work on the streets keeping an eye out for kids, trying to stop gang fights by visiting shooting victims in hospitals, trying to head off retaliation.

Ultimately, however, the essence of this "new" policing, which may in fact be the "oldest" because of the intimate police/community connection, must be felt by each individual officer, held to as belief, not just practice.

Jhukuruin Cole, a young African American male, had recently joined the police force in Memphis, TN. He shared his thoughts as a member of the Youth Panel at the National Forum on Youth Violence Prevention's Annual Summit, held in Washington, DC, in May, 2015. After I heard him speak, I wanted to talk with him. No, I *had* to talk with him. Why was this promising young man joining the police force right in the teeth of national hostility toward the police? It was difficult to pry this slender young man with a bow tie away from his fellow members of the summit's youth delegation. We found a quiet space, if only for about fifteen minutes. He confessed that his background was "somewhat spotty," but that he was "blessed" with mentors, one of whom took him to homeless shelters where they both volunteered. Another mentor paid for his first suit and another paid for his application to the University of Memphis. "They cared," he told me. "I saw caring. I felt I had to give something back." Memphis Police Chief Toney Armstrong and Major Newell played key roles. They "decided to take a chance on me. Kinda took me under their wings. I had to prove to them and myself that they didn't make a mistake. I never worked so hard in my life. I passed the tests." Jhukuruin speaks of the rigorous physical and academic training. "People think it's easy is to be a police officer. It's not."

Jhukuriun now serves as an officer in the Memphis Police Department. But how does his role as law enforcement officer fit with his past, how is his new role seen by the guys from his old neighborhood? How does it fit with him, his life? Jhukuriun paused for a long time before giving a beautifully ingenuous answer. His answer referred neither to policy, nor to a police manual. His answer grew right from his personal experience. "Well, I really don't call it enforcement," he said slowly. "Yes, sometimes you have to do what you have to do. But to me the work is more like protection. You see I know what it's like to go to school scared. Kids getting bullied. Kids joining gangs so they won't get hurt. Makes me feel real good to know that the kids feel safe going to school when I'm there. They should be able to play. It's hard to play when you're scared. It's really hard to be a kid. I don't want it to be hard."

He continued, touching the central nerve, the heart of law enforcement's slow change in America. "I talk to the kids. I get their trust. Then they can tell me what's going down, at school or in the park." Knowledge of the community, caring for the community, trust building and protection come first. Enforcement, if necessary, last.

"I've had kids tell me that it would help if I showed up at such and such a place or in school. And I do."

RESOURCES

- The Advancement Project's Urban Peace Program, the Community Safety Partnership, and "Relationship-Based Policing: Achieving Safety in Watts" (http://advancementprojectca.org). For additional information or technical assistance, slee@urbanpeaceinstitute.org.
- Police Foundation (http://policefoundation.org/about): advancing policing through innovation and science.
- President's Task Force on 21st Century Policing (http://www.cops.usdoj.gov/policingtaskforce)
- The Office of Community Oriented Policing Services (http://www.cops.usdoj.gov) (COPS Office) is a component within the United States Department of Justice.
- The National Initiative for Building Community Trust and Justice (http://trustandjustice.org) is designed to improve relationships and increase trust between minority communities and the criminal justice system.
- Santa Rosa Police Department 2014 Annual Report: "We are committed to making Santa Rosa a safe place to live, work and play" (http://ci.santa-rosa.ca.us/SiteCollectionImages/AnnReport.2014.pdf)

CHAPTER 10

Welcome Home?
The Challenges of Jail to Job

"You don't know what it's like when you're out, man. You're out but you ain't out because you're in jail in your head. You ain't never had to do anything in jail, just not get into trouble. Here it's all on you. Tell you how bad it is: first six months I was out I still put toilet paper on the seat. And I still wore slippers in the shower—at my home! You don't want to slip in the shower in jail. Didn't talk to anybody. Didn't trust anybody. If you're nice in jail you drop your guard and you can get hurt real bad."

- Daren, CEO participant

"When I got home from jail, I just stayed in my room for three days. I didn't know how to work a cell phone. I didn't have nowhere to go, no focus, no plan. Didn't move. Scared. Everything was foreign. A different planet. I finally got up the courage to take the subway. I felt like a tourist. I bought a card for $2.50, but I couldn't get out because I owed twenty-five cents more. I was too scared to talk to anybody. I was sure I was going to be rearrested and sent back to jail for twenty-five cents. Sometimes you just want to go back to prison."

- Caine, CEO participant

POLICY

We work so hard to strengthen our communities—from early intervention, to corrections, to rehabilitation. We clean up and address the threats to our communities, but then, if our mission is whole, we must also welcome our offenders back into the community, offer them training, trust, patience and love. All too often this last step, the last wound to heal, is neglected. As if they were ghosts, we see parolees return to their communities with no road map, no prospects and nowhere to go but back—back to the only thing they know, the thing that brought them to prison in the first place. This is the last mile in truly building communities that don't produce crime. We can't give up on the last mile, nor can we naively believe a hug and a handshake are going to do the job with this population—the most volatile, the least supported, those most at risk of crime. We need to walk this last mile together—it's a tough policy and a hard road, but one group is rewriting the roadmap for us all and helping our offenders walk boldly into a brighter future.

WALKING

CEO: The Center for Employment Opportunities

The Center for Employment Opportunities helps those transitioning from life behind bars to life in an unfamiliar, overwhelming, often unwelcoming place—society—find and keep jobs: and not just any ex-offenders, but the tough ones, ones with extensive criminal justice histories—an average of seven prior convictions, five years in state prison, 70 percent with prior arrests for violent offenses, and 51 percent who had been convicted of a violent offense.

Incubated by New York's prestigious Vera Institute, CEO was spun off as a separate entity in 1978. Supported originally by the City of New York Department of Housing Preservation and Development and the State Division of Parole, CEO's growth and expansion was catalyzed by federal funding such as the American Recovery and

Reinvestment Act (ARRA) and the Social Innovation Fund. More recently, CEO was involved in one of the first "Pay for Success" (PFS) programs in the country that helped the organization serve an additional 2,000 individuals. The PFS arrangement is a version of the Social Impact Bond financing model where investors fund a program with demonstrated results. The program is monitored and rigorously evaluated, and, if mutually agreed upon goals are reached or exceeded, the government then pays back the investors—potentially with a margin. The pay points are based on projected "savings" e.g., lowered prison costs, the government is achieving based on successful outcomes. According to researchers, the success of PFS has less to do with investors recouping their investment, but is more about government accountability and focusing resources on results rather than reimbursements. CEO is fully committed to collecting and assessing data in real time—daily.

Expectations—and results—are high, so the rigorous performance requirements of the PFS agreements are the norm for CEO. It's a perspective that has served the CEO staff—and their participants— well.

CEO's vision, written in bold letters on the wall, greets the visitor when entering CEO's headquarters at 50 Broadway, the heart of Wall Street, the tip of Manhattan. It is straightforward and eminently clear:

"Anyone returning from prison who wants to work has the preparation and support needed in order to find a job and stay attached to the labor force."

CEO's Chief Executive Officer, Sam Schaeffer, former Director of Economic Development for Senator Chuck Schumer, expands the vision. "We want to break the grip of incarceration and the cycle of poverty," Sam tells me. "Poverty?" I ask. "We have to realize the impact of poverty on recidivism," he says, "the recidivism measure is not enough, nor is it the money alone. We aim to build connections between people returning home, their communities and our economy. It's a complete break in lifestyle: showing wives and other family members that they can turn their lives around; getting to work at 6:00 and coming back to their families at the end of the day." Sam stresses the normal, not the exotic: "Getting up, going to work, being on time, getting a check, starting a career. Seem simple?" he asks. "It's not. For most of our enrollees it a total change in how to do life."

Getting and cashing a check seems so easy, so normal. "No, for me it's not. I have five kids. I'm that old, and I never cashed a check before. I almost didn't cash my first check. Is this real? Is this me? I just stared at it," said CEO participant Kendal. Kendal, I thought, had begun to embody "currency" in both senses of the word—currency as money and the currency of a fledgling ability to deal with the "normal" world. "I thought maybe, just maybe I belonged here," he reflects.

Striking Results

In 2004, the federal Department of Health and Human Services contracted with Manpower Demonstration Research Corporation (MDRC) to evaluate programs serving the hard to employ. MDRC utilized a rigorous random assignment evaluation research design – called a "Gold Standard Evaluation" because of its use of a control group. CEO over-recruited more people than it could serve, randomly assigning participants either to full CEO services or just to pre-employment training classes. MDRC followed study participants for three years. CEO came out on top. It showed a reduction in recidivism by 16 to 22 percent, increased employment in the first year of the study with some gains fading after the first year, and striking cost savings—total benefits of up to $3.85 for every $1.00 spent on the program, benefits in the form of reduced criminal justice expenditures and the value of services provided by CEO participants to government agencies in transitional job work sites.

CEO's Core Structure

CEO sends its new enrollees to five days of training in "soft" work skills—how to work with others, how to behave in a workplace, showing up on time, dressing appropriately, being groomed.

The enrollees then move to the "transitional jobs" part of program. Here, they work four days a week doing maintenance or janitorial work mostly in city agencies, some at John Jay College. On day five they meet in CEO's offices with their "job coach" who goes over their grades for the week. Grades, given daily by the Site Supervisors who oversee crews of 5-7 people, cover five basic work behaviors: Cooperation with Supervisors, Effort at Work, On-Time, Cooperation with Co-Workers, and Personal Presentation. Gratification is instant: if the day's grade warrants it, participants received a paycheck that day.

On average, participants work 30-75 days on a transitional job (TJ) site prior to a full-time job placement. This is generally spread over a 2-3 month period. Participants placed in a full-time job receive 12 months of job retention services such as work habits, money management, attitude and attendant issues such as education, drug abuse, and housing.

Parole, CEO's "essential partner," handles referrals to other needed services, especially those in the areas of mental health and education.

If they do well in the transitional part of the program, which lasts anywhere from 30-75 days, they become "CEO licensed," which means job-ready. CEO has placed thousands in jobs—as truck drivers, in restaurants, and in businesses large and small. CEO is trusted by those who hire CEO graduates. A CEO license means something. CEO's staff of Job Developers look for openings, try to create openings and make every effort to convince the hiring agency that a particular CEO graduate is indeed job ready and that CEO will continue to provide requisite support services.

"Why would businesses hire these guys with heavy records?" I ask Sam. "It's changed dramatically," he asserts. He points to "Ban the Box" legislation where city agencies that have submitted themselves to this law, cannot ask an applicant about criminal justice history until well into the job application process. "In addition," he notes, "the left and the right side of the political spectrum are coming together on this, the right often for religious reasons and the left because inmates have paid their dues, and deserve to work." Sam also believes that the national conversation has changed, that both the government and businesses realize that the nation suffers from hundreds of thousands who are out of work, and hundreds of thousands of jobs that need filling. The United States needs workers. "These individuals are suffering, and the nation is suffering," said Sam.

The CEO Difference

Many transitional jobs programs exist for ex-offenders returning home. Trying to get beyond the structure, I ask Sam what values, what principles undergird the work of CEO. He cites three: integrity, flexibility and "normalcy." "First of all, integrity: we do what we say. We're honest about who we are, and we keep learning. We process client information daily. We collect reports on each CEO client every day. CEO enrollees get the same message from each staff member. CEO staff are all different. We come from different backgrounds, have different skills, but we're as accountable and transparent as we expect CEO clients to be. We assess how our clients are doing, and how we're doing."

"And we're flexible," he continues. "If they've got appointments during the day, let's say drug abuse counseling, anger management or working on their high school equivalency, we'll put them on the evening shift. And if they've got night obligations, they'll work the day shift." I ask about the location here on Wall Street, a sliver of the Hudson River seen from his office window glinting in the distance, hoards of people on the streets, tourists mixing with crisply dressed businessmen and women. "But why here? Why not in the Bronx or Brooklyn, closer to where these guys live?" I ask. "That's the point!" he responds. "We want CEO enrollees to feel like they're coming to a job, that they're employees, which they are. And because this lower part of Manhattan is such a transportation hub, we can be reached easily from any part of the city. They're on the subway with people who are going to work, getting off the subway mixed in with people all headed for their jobs. This is an introduction to work: they work, they get paid, they get supported. And it's a little deeper: they know we're here for them."

From the Clients' Perspective

I asked three CEO enrollees what was different about this program. I said I was certain that they had been in many programs, been the subject of many "services." But what was the heart, what really distinguished CEO? What made the difference for them? Kendal used the metaphor of a jigsaw puzzle, noting that CEO puts "all the pieces together," and that returning inmates have many holes in their puzzles, so many holes to fill: "The other programs just give you a metro card and a job. That's it. There are so many missing pieces in our lives, resumes, appointments, and how to take an interview without sweating to death. They helped me put those pieces in and I started feeling normal."

Caine, who had poignantly described sitting alone at home, afraid to go outside following his release, pointed to "structure, to a steady pace every day. I needed structure because prison has structure, predictability." Caine also noted that there is something different about the CEO staff. "They really want your best interest." Kendal said that the staff gave him purpose, "a desire to live confidently. I've been shot, but I'm learning trust. They taught me caring." Daren picked up on Kendal's theme about the nature of CEO's staff: "What I love about these people here is this: They care about you more than you care about yourself. They work so hard." Cain spoke of "an open mind, that $10.00 an hour is not beneath me. At first I thought it was. But it's a start. A ledge, beginning of a purpose, a start."

I spoke of altruism, of giving back as one of the five key resiliency factors. Did they feel giving back made or would make a difference? Kendal said that CEO gave him the confidence to speak to others. He now serves as a motivational speaker in a youth facility. Daren noted that inmates come out "mistrusting...ready to stab...cussing all the time." And that, "I've changed because this staff has given so much to me. CEO has given so much to me; I want to represent them well."

I asked about the peer support, whether there was an AA or Weight Watchers dimension to CEO, because CEO participants are not dropped into a regular workplace, but organized into work crews— something highly unusual, as association with other inmates is usually not permitted by parole. They eat together, work together and take coffee breaks together. Such "togetherness" can lead to a better work environment, can alter something deeper, something harder to get at, trust, trust almost totally obliterated in jail. Each spoke of mutual support, the constant flow of information such as where jobs might be, or housing, or where to get clothes and what was still difficult for them to "get it together." "One guy started to break, a guy with a beard," recalled Kendal. "He cried. I held him." Cain observed that the group "gets encouraged by others who are beginning to make it. And we can help the guys who aren't ready."

Trust, love, mutual support, confidence, follow through: all hard to quantify, and all, according to the guys, essential parts of what makes CEO different.

The Future

I asked Sam whether the numbers overwhelm him—25,000 New York inmates and across the nation, 600,000 inmates are released from prison back to their communities every year. "I am daunted and I'm galvanized, challenged," he responded. "We've got to break the work into pieces, get some jobs off the banned list, plug into social innovation funding, realize that we've got a catalytic role, get other localities to pick up the work." CEO operates programs in Albany, Binghamton, Buffalo, and Rochester, New York; in Oakland, San Bernardino, and San Diego, California; Philadelphia, Pennsylvania; and in Oklahoma City and Tulsa, Oklahoma.

Sam believes that the national conversation has changed dramatically, that "this is a political and cultural moment that we have to seize." What does the seizure look like? Sam is very clear. Future work will occur in three areas—growth, making changes in policy, and continuous quality improvement:

- "We can and will grow. Our programs have been and will continue to be replicated.
- Policy, meaning securing funding for what works, prying open the large budgets of Corrections, and altering systems, such as licensing bans, jobs closed off for ex-offenders, rules about association, that sort of thing, and
- Work internal to us. Quality. Continuous learning. For instance, we know that huge participant gains in year one can taper off. We didn't have a Recidivism Coordinator, and now we do. We once ran a GED program, and we didn't run it very well. Running an educational program is not our thing. Training and getting returning offenders jobs is. We spun off our GED work, sticking to what we do best."

Big Strides One Day at a Time

Caine will stick with his $10.00 per hour job and, when ready, will return to working on his degree in Sports Medicine.

"I'm on a mission," said Daren vehemently. "I want to be a conductor in the transportation system at $16.80 an hour. And I have an interview in April when they're going to post openings." But this is only a proximate goal for Daren. "My duty is to give back. I was the black sheep in my family. I want to be part of the change." His vision is large: "Country's a mess, kids raising kids, no community helping, no authority, no caring. I'm interested in childhood development, too. But I'm going to help because I've been there."

Kendal's father and uncle are licensed plumbers, and Kendal is on the path to get his license. But, like Daren, that's only his proximate goal, what the outside world sees. His real mission lies deep: "I want to show my family that I can get up early, go to work and come back with a paycheck. I want my kids to be proud of me. I want to show them the way. I want them to hug me at the end of every day."

RESOURCES

- The Center for Employment Opportunities (http://ceoworks.org/)
- MDRC (http://www.mdrc.org) is a non-profit, nonpartisan education and policy research organization.
- National Responsible Fatherhood Clearinghouse (https://fatherhood.gov/content/nrfc-promising-practices) is an initiative that serves fathers involved in the criminal justice system.
- Knowledge Development Centre Research Report: *Ex-offenders as Peer Volunteers: Promising Practices for Community-based Programs* (http://sectorsource.ca/sites/default/files/resources/files/JHoward_ExOffenders_Report.pdf)

CHAPTER 11

Comprehensive Strategies:

All are Affected, All Must Play a Part

"People break silos not because anyone ordered them to,
but because they saw the light."

- Mario Maciel

Director, Mayor's Gang Prevention Task Force,

San Jose, California

On its face, it sounds almost obvious: stopping violence and building community means everyone working together in concert at every step along the way. Easy to say. Harder to do. Much harder. But infinitely more effective and long lasting. Communities are organisms. The cancer of violence must be treated as just that. In this way, we could look at a coordinated plan that connects prevention, intervention, enforcement and reentry, as the healing equivalents of preventative care, early treatment, surgery to remove/repair what you must, and remission—a reclaiming of the body as one's own. Recovery relies on all of these—whether community or cancer—and requires a team of healers, "surgeons," and caregivers working as one. This is where our paths come together, where our policy walk becomes our collective, coordinated march.

Police alone cannot solve our communities' youth violence problem. Police do not parent, educate, or provide jobs for a city's youth. Arresting our way out of the problem is neither sensible nor cost effective. Poverty, poor schools, family collapse, few places where youth can drop their guard and be nurtured or have fun, and the easy availability of guns have little to do with law enforcement. Relying on police alone takes everybody else off the hook—and simply doesn't work.

The ramifications of violence ripple well beyond the individual—it affects a jurisdiction's basic functioning. Community members retreat in fear. Civic participation dries up. Businesses pack up and leave. Health care and criminal justice costs soar, property values decrease and kids fear going to school. Studies show that those who do attend school are so concerned about safety that learning is severely compromised.

POLICY

Violence doesn't discriminate. As all are affected, so all must play a part in prevention. A comprehensive, citywide plan combining prevention, intervention, enforcement and prisoner reentry must be forged—a plan that includes all key governmental and civic entities through multidisciplinary partnerships where each partner is committed to taking specific actions. Forging that must include the voices of those most affected by crime. Prevention services might include family strengthening and early childhood education; intervention could include mentoring and school reengagement strategies; enforcement might address crime "hotspots" and re-stationing of police officers; and reentry might include housing, job training and mental health services for returning offenders.

Reentry programs are an essential part of the whole. Youth and young adults returning from prison usually return with few marketable skills, some with mental health and drug issues, and most return to fragile, mistrusting communities. Those deeply involved in the criminal justice system are most prone to returning to it.

Having the diverse program elements folded into a single, coordinated plan has significant, if not dramatic, policy and political implications. When crime rises, a frightened public usually demands more enforcement. Prevention efforts are slow to show results. When fear rises, investment in prevention drops. Unless a city has a comprehensive plan. A comprehensive plan brings traditional and non-traditional allies together: If cuts are imminent, it is not only the prevention community advocating for continuing prevention funding, such as universal pre-school, but also the affected community itself, the police, public health, or even the business community arguing that prevention services must remain.

Launching a citywide, comprehensive plan is tough work. To do this work, a city must bring to the table representatives from organizations that have different mandates, different goals, and different views about how to deal with the issue of violent crime. Essential and diverse, partners include education, enforcement, public and mental health, child welfare, courts, probation, and parole, philanthropic organizations, business and faith and community-based organizations. Without collective, coordinated action and cross agency partnerships, the comprehensive effort devolves to a collection of scattered programs—in other words, business as usual. It takes a strong mayor or city manager to bring such diverse entities to the table and to keep them there.

"And don't forget the community voices," asserts Cora Tomalinas, citizen activist and member of San Jose's Gang Prevention Task Force. Cora, who serves on several community boards—First Five, Silicon Valley Education Foundation, and Sacred Heart Community Services to name a few—has never lost her insistent community voice. "Without the voices of pain," Cora says heatedly, "the educated ones, the elite will go off on their own." Her message, consistent, firm and lovingly confrontational, is clear: "The Task Force must hear from the mommies and the daddies living in our high crime areas. They're the ones whose kids are afraid to go to school. They're the ones who've had their kids shot. They're the ones who work three jobs to keep bread on the table."

WALKING

It takes a rare person to manage a strategy with so many moving parts. Mario Maciel who runs the Mayor's Gang Prevention Task Force in San Jose, is one of these rare ones. He directs what is probably the most successful comprehensive violence prevention effort in the nation.

"I didn't find the work, the work found me," says Maciel who grew up in Gilroy, CA, a small agricultural community famous as "The Garlic Capital of the World." But, as the oldest child of a migrant family from Mexico, he recalls riding the school bus suffering the searing racial comments and being embarrassed about, "being brown and not wearing the right clothes. I lived on the wrong side of town. Trouble was all around us. It came close to home, into our home. My brother got caught up in it and still serves time—eight more years to go. I was groomed to take over at a young age but I had made up my mind early on I wasn't going that route."

He didn't. The first in his family to go to college, Mario initially planned to study psychology, "to become a psychologist or a social worker so I could help figure these kids out." He graduated, taking a job working with gang kids in Gilroy. He concluded that psychology might distance him from the "kids who looked just like me." Mario didn't want clinical distance. He wanted to be on the street, engaged. "I knew the roads they were on and I knew those roads led to disaster. It broke my heart because I knew where they'd wind up – dead or in jail. I discovered that I was good: I could tell them how hurt or wrong they were, and I could do it with respect. They trusted me."

He saw "transformations" that stoked his growing commitment to youth headed to or already in trouble. "Kids came to my tattoo removal program not able to look me in the eye. They couldn't go into stores without being targeted, watched as 'other.' Too many times people are judged by their covers, rather than their content. When they got their 'tatts' off, they could look me, and the entire world, in the eye without shame. They were transformed. I can't tell you how many of these formerly 'tatted' kids went on to college or to get good jobs. I'm sure that nearly all of them went on to live better and more peaceful lives."

In his work today, Mario both embraces and embodies the Comprehensive Strategy Approach. "Enforcement's an essential part of the strategy, but," Mario warns, "when we enforce, we create a vacuum, and something's going to fill it. And what fills it is usually more trouble." Thus, he argues for "intervention" programs such as mentoring, job training and truancy reduction strategies for those who would fill "the vacuum." He argues passionately for "holistic" approaches. He also points to the danger of over-reliance on either end of the spectrum—prevention or enforcement. "We've got to support families and protect our youngest from violence. But if that's all we do, it won't work because prevention results take years to see—healthier kids, kids staying in school, youth going on to careers." He maintains that the public has every right to demand safety, and that the public will not support prevention programs unless they can feel safe—kids going to school without fear, people able to get to work. "Everything has to move forward together."

"You see," asserts Mario, "we've got to have everybody. You can call it 'multi-faceted' or 'holistic,' but what it really means is that we're in it together, sharing resources, creating new approaches, feeding off each other's energy, supporting each other." Without support from the top, consistent support over time, "it will collapse." Because San Jose has been at it so long, Maciel believes the comprehensive approach is now engrained as a part of the city's culture. "It would be extremely difficult for a new administration to eliminate it. The community wouldn't let it happen," he says. "Cops rely on our citizens, the faith community, service providers and street workers to help."

"And you've got to have support from the bottom," maintains Cora. "This can't be top down only," she continues. "The community must be an equal stakeholder. They're in the trenches. They're the ones who told the city that offenders returning to their community have no support. They're the ones who told city councilors that young women were joining gangs in increasing numbers, and that the Task Force had to do something about it. And if they feel heard," she says, "they'll take more responsibility."

The commitment is not rhetorical: The Mayor's Gang Prevention Task Force meets monthly to review progress and the city council allocates roughly $5M annually to support the city's comprehensive efforts. "And people really like being together, being part of something larger," says Mario. He believes deeply that the Mayor's Gang Prevention Task Force is integrally woven into San Jose's civic fabric. "It's here to stay."

Sustaining the Effort

When asked about the challenges he faces, Mario doesn't hesitate. "Easy," he says. "Keeping it all together. Juggling everything. Affirming everyone. Holding people accountable to something larger than their individual mandates." He notes the importance of the "relational glue" that transcends any formal memorandum of understanding (MOU). The work and partnership must transcend the contract. "People must be affirmed, visited, their complaints heard and they must be publicly praised. Kids' faces and stories and our vision must be kept in front of everyone."

Cora echoes Mario's thoughts. "What holds us together are the relationships. At our annual retreat we work hard, but we have fun, too. People know about each other's work and agencies, but they also know their personal journeys, their families. I don't know any task force across the country that hug each other like we do. When we call each other, we don't ask for a title, a 'director' or 'president,' we ask for the person by name."

And that's one of the core reasons the Mayor's Gang Prevention Task Force has not only stayed but remained vital for over 25 years. Critical to that success is the fact that the City's violence prevention overall plan is refreshed every three years as it adapts to changing demographic and economic realities. The plan stays vital. Case in point: The titles of the city's major plans attest to the evolution, if not revolution: "Project Crackdown," with an almost exclusive focus on enforcement, was the city's first. More titles followed; "Neighborhood Revitalization Strategy" and "Strong Neighborhoods Initiative," which focused on building community through neighborhood organizing and empowerment. The 2011-2013 plan "Action, Collaboration, Transformation" was refreshed via the 2015-2017 plan "Trauma to Triumph" with a goal "to foster hope and break the cycle of youth violence."

Presence in the city budget makes a difference. Resources support the wide range of programs needed to sustain a comprehensive effort. Flexibility is also a key. The city awards a slew of contracts to address needs across the continuum of prevention, intervention, enforce and reentry. Contractor performance is evaluated. Over time needs change and in turn contracts and interventions change. It is a paradox: sustainability seems directly connected to flexibility and change.

About five years ago while pondering why things last, why they are sustained, I pressed Cora about her view of the future. "You've just elected a new mayor," I said. "What makes you think he'll continue the Task Force?" Cora admonished me. "Jack, you don't understand. It's not his Task Force. It's ours. The community's." Her assertion doubles back to the point that if the work is not owned and appreciated by the community, there will be no political push to keep it. "Community members will fight for something they own and that they feel works. I've seen meetings where 200 community members show up."

San Jose articulates its vision in its citywide plan:

"Safe and healthy youth connected to their families, schools, communities and their futures."

A vision buttressed by its mission:

"We exist to ensure safe and healthy opportunities for San Jose's youth, free of gangs and crime, to realize their hopes and dreams, and become successful and productive in their homes, schools and neighborhoods."

Mario believes that if people come to the table under duress and only to honor a contract, it won't work. "They've got to believe in the mission. And they've got to know their part. It's my job to remind them of the vision and how essential their part is," he says. He's busy constantly supporting, encouraging, cheerleading, problem solving. Mario helps implement the vision. Cora and her "mommies and daddies" give it moral voice.

The challenges are partly structural, jurisdictional, and territorial. Cities in America hold most of the violence problems. But the counties—child welfare, health and human services, probation, courts, hospitals—hold most of the resources, "My work is to persuade them to come aboard and to share resources," he asserts. "The mayor can bring the city to the table, but he has no authority over the county or the school system. That's tough."

"People break silos," according to Mario, "not because anyone ordered them to, but because they saw the light," subscribed to the vision, saw their role in a larger context, saw themselves as part of the whole. Training and support are constant. "It seems someone in the partnership is having a training every week. And we all get invited to each other's trainings."

Successes

While Mario can cite crime rates dropping or holding steady, high school dropout rates improving, and the fact that San Jose won't abandon the approach—it's embedded—he, curiously, or maybe not so curiously, keeps pointing to the quality of the relationships, new people who've come aboard, and the faces, always the faces, "the 200 kids who stayed with the Summer Jobs Program," and the "hard core homies" who just graduated from Voc Ed with trades and jobs. Or simply the "shorties"—young ones playing handball, shooting hoops, or playing soccer at San Jose's late night gyms.

He urges his peers to remind the city and the city council about the return on investment: the number of kids graduating, the number of people who didn't go back to prison, the number of parks made safe, the drop in homicides. Make sure everybody makes specific commitments—to specific tasks—"and then make sure to hold them accountable and communicate the wins," he asserts.

Personal Advice

"Take care of yourself," are Mario's first words. "Keep yourself together. Remember to heal yourself." His work might include responding to a shooting at 2:00 am to attending a clergy breakfast at 8:00 am to testifying before the city council later in the day. "And when the shit hits the fan, I'm there." So, he says, "you've got to go dark, turn off your phone, get away. Do whatever sustains you," he suggests. "Be with your kids, fish, go away and turn off your phone. If you don't take care of yourself, you're no good to anyone."

"Never lose sight of why you're doing the work, the moral imperative," he urges. "And don't lose the kids' faces." That's not easy because doing what Maciel suggests means you won't be home for dinner. And a child's shattered body or an inconsolable mother may not be faces everyone can endure.

"Never stop learning," he says excitedly. "If you feel you know everything, you're done." He relishes the dynamic nature of the work. Unlike most cities, he and the city leaders rewrite the citywide plan every few years. The plan must respond to an ever-changing city. "It keeps us fresh. Things change. New people come in. New jobs may open up or close down. A new gang might have formed. The proportion of our work always changes, sometimes more prevention, sometimes more enforcement and hotspot policing, and sometimes more intervention," he says. He believes that re-planning, rethinking, and recreating the plan keep things moving, keep the vision in front of all.

He advises his peers in other cities to know their partners' mandates and to know each partner personally, their hopes, fears and commitments. "Believe me," he stresses, "MOUs don't do it. Relationships do. You've got to believe. They've got to believe. My job, my colleagues' jobs? Get others to believe. Make them feel special. Let them know the critical role they play, their essential place in the whole picture."

"And you've got to believe that you're lucky to do this work," Mario concludes. "Yeah, sometimes I almost hit the wall. Then I look at my city and county partners who are not only my colleagues but my friends. Then I pinch myself."

Cora feels the same way. "I could never not be involved. I work closely with people in the trenches who would give their lives and their love for others. I've seen a lot of pain. But I've seen a lot more love. How could I stay away from these wonderful people?"

A Blueprint: Lessons from the CCVPN

The comprehensive strategy approach began in California in 2007 as the California Cities Violence Prevention Network (CCVPN). Thirteen cities joined, including all of California's largest and those from the south, including San Diego and Los Angeles, and from the north, including San Francisco and Sacramento. In 2010, at the direction of President Obama, the National Forum on Youth Violence Prevention (the Forum), modeled on the CCVPN, was established to build a national commitment to addressing youth violence through comprehensive planning and action. The Forum intends to create a vibrant national network of federal and local stakeholders who, through the use of multidisciplinary partnerships, balanced approaches and data-driven strategies, strengthen communities so that they may better prevent violence and promote the safety, health and development of the nation's youth. At the time of this writing, comprehensive strategies are underway in the Forum cities of Baltimore, Boston, Camden, Chicago, Cleveland, Detroit, Long Beach, Louisville, Memphis, Minneapolis, New Orleans, Philadelphia, Salinas, San Jose, and Seattle.

The Structure of Strategy:
Essential Elements of a Comprehensive Plan

Leadership - City and county leaders—mayor, chief, school, public health—must back the comprehensive planning/action process. Ideally, leadership should take three forms: moral—a commitment that this level of violence in their city will stop; conceptual participation in the planning process; bureaucratic—a willingness to change how city agencies do business. Comprehensive planning rests on the belief that violence will not be reduced unless all community entities are galvanized to act. The leadership job is to rally the entire city—public and private, civic and governmental—focusing, altering and coordinating its varied capacities and mandates.

Inclusive Planning & Reporting - Planning must stretch horizontally across city and county (e.g., probation, public health, child welfare) agencies, and vertically, deep into the community, especially those communities most affected by violence. Their input can be solicited via surveys, community and school meetings and the like. Such fact-gathering cannot stop at the gathering: beleaguered communities have been promised a great deal, and they are wary. Those who gather the facts must get back to the community, pointing to aspects of the plan where the community's voice was heard. Community members must be included as stakeholders, not as a benighted group being "done to".

Grout - Involving all key partners to address a wide variety of topical issues is part of the work. The danger is that all will continue to operate in silos. Thus the core challenge facing Forum cities is to establish robust interconnections between programs and priorities—and a willingness to codify those connections and communicate freely. Think of tiles: tiles include those of different participating entities such as police, public health and the faith community. Tiles also include varied topics, such as family support, mentoring, job training, hot spot policing. Without grout, tiles collapse: they lack cohesion, integration, connection. "Grout" in this context might include a Memorandum of Understanding, changes in local codes/ordinances, changes in state law, local tax initiatives, restrictions on gun sales, changes in school discipline policy, changes in public transportation routes, etc., to support the common comprehensive strategy for violence prevention. Cora would view these types of grout as important, very important, but not essential. "What really holds us together, Jack, are the relationships. It doesn't mean we don't argue. We do. But we also know how each of us cares. And we are there for each other, pulling for each other, helping each other."

Implementation Clarity - In addition to the standard vision, goals, objectives (and if desired, core values or principles), the plan must specify who will do what and by when, i.e., responsible party and timeline. Commitment must be specific, not rhetorical. Examples of city plans can be found in the Resources section of this chapter.

Governance - This aspect of comprehensive planning cannot be emphasized enough. A broad-based entity is essential, one that tracks plan progress, holds people accountable, ensures health of the partnerships (including communication strategies) and refreshes the plan. Examples of "entities" include the Community Alliance for Safety and Peace in Salinas, California, Camden, New Jersey's City Forum on Youth Violence Prevention and Boston's Youth Violence Prevention Collaborative. Without strong governance, comprehensive planning devolves to a loose collection of uncoordinated programs that cannot achieve the exponential impact of a coordinated whole. Governance allows the serendipitous to occur: need tutors for third graders? The faith community might step up. Need mentors for at risk youth? Police academy graduates might help. And if the governance is robust, key governmental and civic organizations don't want to be left out. It's the place to be, as the city redesigns its approach to crime and violence, changes its norms. Ideally, to manifest total citywide commitment to the comprehensive effort, the mayor, city manager or someone in the city structure with power should chair the meetings and help drive the process.

Sufficient Staff - Comprehensive work necessitates staff sufficient to oversee the planning process, plan implementation, governance, data collection and intra and extra-partnership communications. Ideally, lead staff should report to the mayor or mayor's designees. If staff leads are buried in the bureaucracy or without sufficient authority, forging partnerships and driving the comprehensive work becomes difficult if not impossible.

Integrated Data - Multiple data sources (e.g., criminal justice, education, child welfare, public health) must be used, and data-sharing agreements signed. Data kept in agency silos means we will never fully know a child: one agency holds education data, another child abuse data, and a third, criminal justice. (Integrated data is discussed more fully in Chapter 12.) Without a full picture, a holistic picture of a child, children will be ill or only partially served, the full extent of their issues unaddressed.

Relationships - Those most prone to victimizing and victimization share one glaring characteristic, namely, disconnection, disconnection from family, school, job, hope. Most come from a long line of broken, mistrusting, even abusive relationships. "Relational" work is often subordinated to program and policy. It shouldn't be. Forging relationships with the wary, mistrusting and angry is both extremely difficult and of utmost importance. In a broken world, who says, "I love you. I won't leave you," to these children? Not many. But they must be found. (The importance of relationships is covered in more depth in Chapter 1, "Hey, Loved One" and Chapter 7, "Community Renewal.")

Assessment/Evaluation - Measures of progress, both process (e.g., number of restorative justice sessions held, passage of a new ordinance, data sharing agreements) and outcome (e.g., reduced number of shootings, increased sense of citizen safety, reduced school dropout rates) must be established.

.

While addressing the most volatile individuals and vulnerable areas, a city must do so in the context of an overall citywide plan that involves everyone. All are affected, all must play a part.

A comprehensive strategy is both complex and promising. The moving parts and egos are many, the funding is often iffy, and a sudden spate of shootings can wound individuals and threaten the commitment to the citywide effort. On the other hand, new partnerships and synergies can and do inspire. Lowered rates of violence, children able to walk to school without fear, or new small businesses opening up in formerly crime-ridden areas infuse energy and hope.

RESOURCES

- National Forum Plans (http://www.youth.gov/youth-topics/ preventing-youth-violence/forum-communities/san-jose)
- Crime Solutions (https://www.crimesolutions.gov/)
- Cities United (http://citiesunited.org) Cities United is a collection of mayors from across the country who have joined in a movement to stop the unprecedented loss of life happening in cities across America.
- Centers for Disease Control Youth Violence Page (http://www.cdc.gov/violenceprevention/youthviolence/)
- The Prevention Institute (http://www.preventioninstitute.org) specifically, *Preventing Violence: A Primer* PI is a nonprofit, national center dedicated to improving community health and well-being by building momentum for effective primary prevention. Primary prevention means taking action to build resilience and to prevent problems before they occur.
- Waller, Irvin, *Smarter Crime Control: A Guide to Safer Futures for Citizens, Communities and Politicians*, New York, Rowman and Littlefield, 2014. Smarter Crime Control provides legislators and journalists with disturbing facts that the U.S. is both the most violent, most punitive and most taxed for criminal justice among advanced nations. The book is inspirational and unique in using U.S. knowledge to identify legislative and funding decisions that would stop both the epidemic of street violence, least punitive and least wasteful on criminal justice among advanced nations— saving thousands of lives and multi-billions of wasted taxes.

CHAPTER 12

Do We Really Know the Children?
The Case for Data Sharing

"I've learned that our siloed systems inhibit us from
really knowing a child."

Lack of data sharing affects kids' lives. I've been working for more almost five decades trying to help keep young people safe and thriving. I've learned that our siloed systems inhibit us from really knowing a child. And, without knowing the child, how can we help? In fact, without truly understanding their circumstance, can we be sure our semi-blinded efforts won't harm? Only a fully formed picture of a child based on all of the information available can lead us to the best intervention, the best support, and an opportunity for healing and hope for the child and his or her community.

POLICY

The absence of effective data-sharing protocols creates enormous obstacles to timely and effective services that have the potential to improve outcomes for children and families.

At the local level, it hobbles those who work with young people and unnecessarily burdens already burdened parents, parents who have to deal with different agencies each with different forms, each usually located in different parts of the city.

A Moral Issue

Such "absence" can even mean the difference between life and death. The stakes are high. I serve as a member of the Department of Justice's National Forum on Youth Violence Prevention's site visiting team. One visit took us to Philadelphia, whose Mayor, Michael Nutter, views data sharing as nothing less than an issue of life and death: "Look," he said, slamming his fist on the table, "we're often faced with situations where we know a youth is about to kill or be killed. We have to rethink all the data and legal issues, because this is not a legal or technical issue. We're talking about saving lives. Data sharing is a moral issue!"

If a child is disruptive in school, the teacher and school social workers may know only that he has a discipline problem. They may not know that the child has suffered abuse at the hands of an "uncle" for several years (information held by Child Protective Services), that his biological father is in prison (information held by the court or probation), or that his brother had been shot on the street a few weeks earlier (information held by the police).

Similarly, if a youth is charged with a juvenile offense, her probation officer may see a requirement of school attendance as in her best interest. What the officer may not know is that her learning disabilities make school a place of personal shame and pain rather than a place where she feels she can get her life back on track.

In *Getting Big Data to the Good Guys*, Stephen Goldsmith and Christopher Kingsley affirm this phenomenon by painting a stark picture of the everyday reality for many educators, social workers, probation officers and others who work with the most vulnerable, asserting that they "...are working in a digital dark age. [For example], with few exceptions:

- Street outreach workers helping a child find emergency shelter cannot determine whether he or she receives psychiatric care or suffers from physical health conditions;

- Juvenile courts cannot access students' academic records, even to verify school attendance and inform judgments; and
- Planning directors cannot track clients' use of services across systems either to coordinate care or to understand the factors and sequence of events that shape a youth's involvement in public systems."

The result is often less effective—or sometimes even counterproductive—interventions for the children and youth who most need our help.

WALKING

San Francisco spends millions of dollars a year to serve a small number of families and young people whose lives have been damaged by poverty and violence. Historically, these services have been fragmented across stove-piped systems, lacking coordination at the level of strategy, case coordination or both.

Dan Kelly, Director of Planning for San Francisco's Human Services Agency, describes the "poles" of service provision for vulnerable families. He illustrates one extreme through the story of his own grandfather, who raised himself on the streets of Philadelphia:

"It was around the year 1900. He ran away from home when he was 9 or 10 years old because of an abusive father. He slept in alleyways, joining other street orphans who erected plywood roofs over their blankets. They took care of each other, raised each other. They had no services. My grandfather only finished the third grade. I often wonder how his life would have been different if he'd had supportive services, and in turn, how my father's life would have been different if his father hadn't been so scarred by trauma." In other words, nobody helped him, nobody knew him.

On the other extreme, Kelly cites an example from his experience as an outreach worker:

"One of the families I worked with was headed by a single mother, who was struggling with her own trauma while raising three sons. Each of the boys was in trouble of some kind. One was on probation; another was in and out of foster care. Each was failing in school. Their housing was in jeopardy. This mother had at least three caseworkers and had to tell her story over and over again to each one, had to make sense of the different bureaucracies, had to figure out what she was supposed to do with the different case plans. This was an isolated, fragile person. She just wanted help, but it was left up to her to figure out the cacophony of services and systems."

"For families," Kelly continues, "this confusion can be overwhelming. Every mother and father, no matter how troubled, wants their child to have a better life. To see a child struggling in school or in the community, and to know that help is available but difficult to find because the systems providing it are scattered and disorganized—that must be profoundly frustrating."

Further, Kelly points out, uncoordinated service delivery has economic consequences—the lack of coordination across the city's systems reduces the power of its investments. Its different programs often serve the same families. Caseworkers, therapists, probation officers, and teachers are too often unable to coordinate their efforts, undermining their effectiveness and creating expensive inefficiencies.

Because of the confusion, not only are clients ill-served (or at least not optimally served), questions about what works for which individuals and families and at what cost remain difficult, if not impossible to answer.

Although a self-described "data geek," it was the families with whom Kelly worked when making his way through college that frame his data work. "I had two and three jobs at a time, starting as a child care worker and graduating to residential treatment and then to case management." Over the years, he has visited homes in every San Francisco neighborhood, conducted outreach in homeless family shelters, and helped parents entangled in the child welfare system get treatment. "So often," he notes, "people working with data have technical proficiency and can uncover trends in the numbers, but often they don't understand the context of how programs work or that lives are not linear, especially when the stress of poverty keeps life at a constant boil."

Perhaps of greatest importance is that danger signals are not shared. As a result, young people, many of whom might have been diverted from trouble or harm, are not identified early on as being at risk.

Data Sharing's Crystal Ball:
San Francisco on the Vanguard

Through strong leadership from the mayor and leaders of city and county agencies, the city and county of San Francisco embarked on a major data-sharing initiative. Balancing the need to improve outcomes for clients and increase efficiency of operations while protecting the confidentiality rights of clients, Dan Kelly and colleagues brought together the top leaders of several public agencies.

After extensive discussions among these leaders about the need to better serve families by sharing information (and a court order), San Francisco's public health, juvenile probation and child welfare agencies forged a memorandum of understanding (MOU) in 2005 that allowed for the pooling of information into a secure database. For the first time, child protective service workers could find out if a child in an emergency situation had a probation officer or a psychiatrist who should be involved in a response plan.

The initial analysis of the shared data stunned Kelly and his colleagues. Through the Shared Youth Database (SYDB), as it became known, Kelly and his team made some important discoveries. About 2,000 high-risk families in the city consumed about half of the resources in child welfare, juvenile probation, and children's mental health systems, and they were likely to live within walking distance of one of seven street corners in the city. As a result of this discovery, San Francisco concentrated services in specific neighborhoods, co-locating services in key public housing developments and community centers.

The mapping strategies through the shared database showed that millions of dollars were being spent on a handful of families, a figure previously unknown as it had been "refracted through different departments and programs." The database led his team to another intriguing finding: children living in the Tenderloin and South of Market areas, the subjects of child welfare reports and school attendance difficulties, were doing less well than children with similar difficulties living in Chinatown. The database opened other questions and challenges such as caseworker coordination and how to understand the "careers" of these families and when best to intervene.

Andrew Wong, an expert in data-sharing strategies, analyzed the data from crossover clients in San Francisco, concluding that those served by multiple systems were at increased risk of committing a serious crime; over half of young people in the city that are involved in multiple service systems have been convicted of or been the victim of a serious crime.

According to Katherine Miller, San Francisco's Assistant District Attorney, there is no mystery: "When a youth shows up in that third system, the clock can't be ticking any faster at that point."

A Difficult Path: Legal & Other Concerns

The task of forging an MOU among the city's probation, public health, and child welfare agencies was arduous and slow. Optimism would sag due to the sudden departure of a champion, or worried lawyers would create delays. At one point, San Francisco's nascent and promising Shared Youth Database team hit a wall.

Initially, a juvenile court judge issued an order, which spurred an MOU covering the sharing of records. After several years, however, the city attorney called into question the juvenile probation department's legal pathway for participating in the shared system, and, out of caution, urged juvenile probation to withdraw from the MOU.

However, the integrated database pointed to a strong need for prevention through early intervention. "We didn't want to wait until a family is far down this road before having these multi-disciplinary conversations," explained Assistant DA Miller. "Thus, the probation department re-entered the agreement."

In April 2015, the school district signed the MOU as a fourth partner, along with probation, public health, and child welfare. Schools will limit data sharing to the students they have already flagged as "at risk" and will pool essential data so that youth can receive effective, efficient, and coordinated services.

The unprecedented MOU among the schools, probation, public health, and child welfare took almost a decade to achieve.

Wong provides this advice for cities that are thinking about or planning to undertake a similar effort: get the right people at the top to drive the issue, get the lawyers to speak with each other in a timely fashion and stay in close communication with agency heads, and have a consultant on board who can help with technical and legal issues.

Kelly brings the issue back to the ground, noting that, other than technology, the greatest challenges are at the casework level. Workers tasked with entering and receiving data need to provide data to caseworkers in a manner that helps them with their cases today, rather than data for research or evaluation purposes alone.

Realizing this, Kelly involves staff in the data-sharing policy discussions to ensure that high-level data-sharing agreements actually help caseworkers do their job better. He asserts that if the shared data doesn't get used in real time to help those in the most need, then none of this makes sense.

Children and youth in care, whether in the criminal justice, mental or child welfare system, often come from chaotic and poorly functioning families and neighborhoods. "Our service 'systems' can be equally chaotic," says Kelly. "The least we owe fragile families and youth is predictability, a somewhat clear path in an often unpredictable and muddled world," he concludes.

Data Sharing the Old Fashioned Way

Cities in the California Cities Violence Prevention Network (CCVPN) have pledged to develop citywide action plans blending prevention, intervention, enforcement and reentry. CCVPN's core strategy rests on the blending and interweaving of strategies, yet data-sharing structures can cripple service delivery efforts.

But most CCVPN's cities, however, found solutions based on a simple concept: those working with troubled youth and families met periodically to discuss specific cases. They were legally permitted to do so assuming that the "client" in question had the potential for self harm or harm to others.

Almost all of the CCVPN cities established both a policy team—usually comprising the mayor, police chief, school superintendent, public health head and others—and a "tech" or "implementation" team made up of those closest to the problems, namely police officers, local school principals, child welfare workers, and probation officers. Through discussions of specific youth and their families, service efficiencies were maximized. It's data sharing the old fashioned way: talking to one another.

Ernesto Olivares, formerly Executive Director of the Mayor's Gang Prevention Task Force in Santa Rosa, and currently Executive Director of CCVPN said, "We found we were stumbling over each other, each different service often coming into the same families from different agency perspectives. We drove the families crazy, and our service delivery was disjointed and ineffective. Our Tech Team made all the difference. It was stunning to watch the natural coordination that began to occur, such as officers working with child welfare with particular attention to children left in the home following the arrest of a parent."

A Long Way to Go

Kelly in San Francisco, while optimistic, recognizes that data sharing is still a work in progress: "Come back in a year and you'll see fundamental changes in how cases are coordinated. Come back in five years and you'll see changes in the lives of at-risk children."

Kelly shares a memory about a young single mother he had accompanied to get her HIV test result, holding her hand as the doctor spoke with her. Kelly now works in a technical data thicket gratified that he can use his analytical interests to better understand and serve San Francisco's families. "But whenever I feel I'm just looking at numbers," he reflects, "I think about that young mother whose hand I once held."

RESOURCES

- National League of Cities: "Sharing Data for Better Results: A Guide to Integrating Data Systems Compatible with Federal Privacy Laws" (http://www.nlc.org/Documents/Find City Solutions/IYEF/Data Sharing for Better Results.pdf)
- HopeMatters.org: "Sharing Data to Improve Life Chances for Children and Youth" (http://hopematters.org/sharing-data-to-improve-life-chances-for-children-and-youth-san-francisco-on-the-vanguard/)
- *Getting Big Data to the Good Guys* (http://datasmart.ash.harvard.edu/news/article/getting-big-data-to-the-good-guys-140)

CHAPTER 13

Restorer of the Streets:

8 Lessons from My Policy Walk

"...policy alone doesn't move me. What happens to a person or a community because of policy does."

To a significant degree, the success of your work depends on the social, economic, and political context in which you operate. You may have little control over these contexts, but at a minimum you must know of them, refer to them as influences on your purpose and work, and, if time and energy permit, advocate for changes. I have found that, in addition to these external forces, there are some eternal truths about the work we do. They push and pull—some seemingly hopeless, others the foundation of hope itself. These seven lessons have, in some respects, been the way markers of my policy walk. Some have fueled my passion, while others have kept me on the path when the road gets rough. I hope you find them helpful on your journey.

1. Structural Issues

There are three fundamental structural issues, each of which has a profound impact on crime and violence. They are no mystery: the media brings them to our attention almost daily.

First, the obscene availability of guns. As I write these final chapters, the nation is reeling from the slaughter of innocents in San

Bernardino, California. This within days of the unimaginable terrorist attacks in Paris. Thousands die each year, hundreds are children. The reality is that until gun loopholes are closed, assault weapons are banned, and rigorous background checks are enforced, easy access to guns will undermine the efforts of those working tirelessly to keep communities and families safe.

Second, poverty. Income inequality, wealth disparity, a widening income gap, wage stagnation—however you look at it—there's something wrong when responsible, hard-working adults managing two jobs simply cannot support a family. We must address the low wage structure, poverty and the cycle of poverty that will be passed down from generation to generation without intervention.

Third, family collapse. More than 50 percent of American births to women under 30 are outside of marriage; notwithstanding the efforts of amazing single parents—usually women—who raise wonderful children, the results are in: children in single parent households do less well. Their life prospects are compromised. Committed single mothers, often with two jobs are simply too exhausted to read to their child every night, especially with multiple children. Tough work schedules mean little time to follow up with services—visits to school, participation in the PTA or court appearances. Policies, such as support for first time mothers, shared parental leave, setting the expectation for male parenting responsibility in a sea of absentee dads, tax codes that reward marriage and social services making every effort to support families and family formation, must shore up this fragile foundation if our work is to take solid root.

2. Crime Contributes to Community Erosion: And Community Building Erodes Crime

Crime creates a morally unacceptable level of community malfunction, even civic collapse. Crime, especially violent crime, claims two victims: an individual robbed, assaulted or shot, and the community now huddled in fear, neighborhood bonds replaced by suspicion and mistrust. Isolation further exacerbates the crime situation as citizens stay home, leaving the streets to those who would do damage: children and teens fear going to and from school; adults fear taking evening jobs or to serve as school volunteers or Little League coaches; local businesses pull up stakes and leave.

In 2006, San Bernardino's Mayor Patrick Morris refused to accept such collapse as a given. He rallied the city bureaucracy, service providers, and the private sector to focus combined efforts on the most crime-ridden, mistrusting area of the city. He launched "Operation Phoenix," which targeted a 20 square-block area in which a wide range of issues were tackled head on—transportation, housing, code violations, enforcement, neighborhood and park blight, lack of recreation, school attendance, and more. In a few short years, the situation changed dramatically. Crime plummeted, but more importantly, civic lifeblood returned. One citizen said, "For years I've been trying to get out of here. Now I want to stay." Another said, "My kids can play safely outside." Said another proudly, "The street lights work. The potholes are filled, and we can use the park."

While Morris brought everything together in a remarkably effective, collective strategy, he realized that, without basic safety, nothing would work: schools could not teach, businesses would flee, citizens would abandon the streets. He realized fully that violence makes communities impossible to function. Thus, enforcement was an essential part of his collective effort.

Felton Earls, at the Harvard School of Public Health (as mentioned in Chapter 7), Robert Sampson, and other researchers at the Project on Human Development in Chicago Neighborhoods compared neighborhoods in terms of social, economic and demographic traits, as well as crime rates. It became clear: those communities with high rates of "collective efficacy" experienced lower crime rates, regardless of their social and economic makeup. This verifies what common sense tells us—a community in which neighbors care about each other and who are actively involved with various civic entities such as schools and block clubs is a safer neighborhood. Earls found stunning anomalies: in places where data suggested that crime should be high, he discovered, because of "collective efficacy," crime rates were low. Thus, crime reduction and community building strategies must be conjoined.

3. Do Not Indict Entire Communities

Thomas Abt, Senior Research Fellow at Harvard's Kennedy School of Government and David Kennedy, Director of the National Network for Safe Communities at the John Jay College of Criminal Justice warn us not to label entire neighborhoods as "bad." Consigning entire neighborhoods to the "bad" category influences how we police them, serve them, see them, engage them. In point of fact, the overwhelming number of its citizens lead good, responsible lives, want the best for their kids, and they want, desperately, to be safe.

Both point to evidence that effective community violence reduction efforts must include, within the context of a citywide plan:

- Place-based interventions that target specific "micro-locations" (could be a street, a handful of families, not an entire neighborhood)
- People-based interventions that focus on high-risk individuals and groups
- Behavior-based interventions that concentrate on behaviors linked to violence, such as carrying firearms and belonging to a gang

4. Fear Leads to Jail

That we over-rely on jails is an understatement. We represent about 5 percent of the world's population and lock up about 25 percent of its prisoners. We lock up roughly 600 people per 100,000, while Canada locks up about 150 per 100,000 and Holland and Japan lock up only 49 and 39 respectively. Yet residents of these nations feel safer than we do. Fear of crime or fear of not getting re-elected often drives these policies.

The older I get, the more I believe that a great deal of criminal justice policy is made by exhaustion or hysteria. We accuse children and teens of short attention spans, but policymakers' attention spans are often shorter—"Slam, bang, prisons—problem solved." The most violent and the most chronic offenders must be off the streets for a time. But many who exist under lock and key are neither violent nor chronic. And most are minorities and most are poor. Severe ethnic disparities exist in sentencing and who actually gets sent to jail. Simplistic sentencing, refusals to invest in restoration and rehabilitation, a policy of avoidance by warehousing: each of these is built not on reasoned analysis, not on lessons from experience, but on reactions grounded in fear by voters and fear of voters.

Elected officials are to some extent victims in this equation. The media stoke fear. If it bleeds, it leads. Even when crime drops, fear is used to stoke the fires, the smoke often obscuring the actual facts. No wonder public discourse is often framed by terror, not by sound policy.

We tend to be wary about our youth, often seeing them as undisciplined, disrespectful, and unfriendly. As noted in Chapter 4, most of our youth are terrific and committed to shaping a decent future for themselves. Yet a small handful of those who get into trouble, a tiny minority, seem to dictate what we do.

What then is our message, our promise to youth? To the extent that public policy is a promise, we have promised young people shelter, schools and health care for about $60,000 per year – in jail. Is this the main promise to the next generation? The trend seems to be one of fear fueled by images, not reality. The promise seems to be, "We are ready for you; we know you will be bad." Why do we predict and prepare for failure? Why do we stand by until that failure happens and then bemoan the investment in hugely expensive responses?

While not being naïve about the most violent, we've got to help shift the context to elicit and celebrate the best in our young people, instead of awaiting trouble and filling prisons in self-fulfilling prophecy.

We spend a great deal of money on corrections—jails—and the results are dismal. The majority of prisoners will return within a year of release. Many states invest more in corrections than in higher education. Again, what is our message to the young? Surely the violent must be off the street for an extended period of time, but those with lower level offenses can be treated in the community: intensive supervision and support, mentoring, restitution and job training are in the long run cheaper and more effective. Change, however, is in the winds; change is evident: some prisons in Texas not being built or even closing, and California releasing low level offenders from jail. A national trend just may be starting.

5. Measures of Success are Changing

While reductions in crime, especially violent crime, serve as the most salient and preferred benchmarks of success, civic measures, some of which were seen in San Bernardino in 2006, are equally, if not more important. New community norms must be established. Crime can be lowered, but, if the community is shaky, not resilient, crime will return. Thus measures of success must include civic well-being, measures such as an improvement in the high school graduation rate, easier access to jobs, neighborhood stores opening, an increase in voluntarism, creation or resuscitation of civic entities such as Neighborhood Watch and block clubs, an increase in property values, and seemingly small measures such as a high school prom being held for the first time and pizza being delivered again to once-embattled communities. Liz Glazer, former assistant U.S. Attorney for Crime Control Strategies in New York City, once said to me, "I intend to help citizens build a community that is resistant to crime so that I don't have to keep returning as a prosecutor."

Keep an eye on and fight for the programs that work, many of which are described in this book. Make every effort to embed such hopeful programs in the wider context of a healthy, vibrant city (not just a city with less crime). Certain programs hold great promise. But those programs in combination with other hopeful programs hold even greater promise.

6. Bureaucrats Have Souls

I've run two large governmental agencies, one on the state level, one on the federal. When accepting the posts, friends warned me about the "bureaucrats." The warnings usually clustered in four areas: they don't work hard, they don't really care, they don't like change, and they will block you at every turn. I have seen these theories in action from both sides of the bureaucratic divide and, with a little understanding, and a little context, bureaucrats can be some of your strongest allies and stalwart staff.

Government agencies aren't easy to run, and the civil servants can obfuscate, delay, and block. But as a leader, I can say that a hefty dose of humility is in order. Many if not most "bureaucrats" joined at one point in their lives spurred in part by high idealism—to save lives as a cop, to help abused children, to make certain research is conducted properly, that numbers are tracked with integrity. While leaders should be unafraid of their own vision, they've got to realize that idealism, perhaps now barnacled over, brought most staff into government service.

Change is difficult. If you want to make changes, staff must know why, and they must share in shaping the change. I recall my first meeting with the new wunderkind head of the Department of Human Services in Massachusetts to whom I reported, a graduate of Harvard Business School and a former senior executive at Vanguard. It was an era when businesses were viewed as saviors of bumbling, inefficient government. The wunderkind at his first meeting unveiled a new table of organization. We fellow commissioners from Public Health, Welfare, Mental Health and Education stared at each other in disbelief. He had every right to make the changes, even to dazzle us with a new chart replete with arrows and color. But he was completely unable to say what difference the changes would make in the lives of those we were pledged to serve. The reorganization chart went nowhere. It got the old bureaucratic block. Why? Because it had no why.

Bureaucrats do have their turf. They are paid to tend that turf well. It is the job of the leader to elicit and affirm why that particular person is doing his or her job, and how that particular piece of turf fits into the whole landscape. In other words, people need—no, crave—meaning. We are a meaning-based species.

But vision must be coupled with clarity about how the work gets done. Otherwise chaos ensues. Bureaucrats tend to be cautious. Change is difficult. After all, they've been tending their garden in the same way for years. When the deinstitutionalization revolution occurred in Massachusetts, a community-based system had not yet been put in place. When I took over as Commissioner of Youth Services, all was chaos. The state's most troubled (and in some cases violent) kids were scattered in programs across the state, freed from the horror of the large and often abusive "training schools"—huge locked institutions right out of the 19th century—in programs new, untested, and, in many cases, unaccountable. In point of fact, we simply didn't know where hundreds of kids were.

To avoid chaos, and not for any sound policy reasons except security alone, there were 75 bills in the Massachusetts legislature to reopen these grotesque institutions. My job: to help build a community-based system from a community-based movement. My vision of the nation's first community-based juvenile justice system had to be conjoined with the hardheaded reality of creating an accountable system, and that system had to have some security for the state's most violent or chronic offenders. We were able to create that system with only 11 percent of the state's most violent or chronic offenders in locked settings, whereas before all youth committed to the Department of Youth Services had been in locked settings. But it took a lot of time, political support, a clear vision, really mission, and an unadorned commitment to system building.

Bureaucrats can vitiate vision, but they can also serve to curb wayward visionaries. When I served President Carter as his Commissioner of the Administration for Children, Youth, and Families, Duncan Adams, a member of the permanent bureaucracy, held a senior advisory post. Tall, courtly, brilliant, and a bird lover, Duncan was my check. "Sir," he once said to me, "I will follow you anywhere, but before that I will tell you if you're taking ACYF over a cliff." It slowly dawned on me. Duncan was not a blocker. Duncan was a good steward.

I had also pledged to the White House and to the head of the Department of Health and Human Services that I would re-examine our mission and hold a staff retreat. The permanent staff, led by Duncan, resisted. "Why?" I kept asking him. "We have the most precious and exciting mandate in government—children and families." He finally fessed up. "Sir," (he always called me sir even though I could have been his son), "we have our current statutes to administer. Our hands are full." "But Duncan," I replied, "these statutes, such as Head Start, didn't arise from nothing, they arose from need, they were created by caring committed people like you." He pondered and said, "One of our problems is that we fall in love with our commissioners, and then they leave us."

We held the retreat. The retreat generated the outline for what became Bill 96-272 the Child Welfare and Adoption Act of 1980, called one of the three most important laws affecting children in the 20th century. Soon after passage and enactment into law, President Carter lost the election, and, a few months later, I with my fellow presidential appointees, exited. "See, you broke our hearts," said

Duncan after the election. "Mine really hurts, too. I adored my job, the best job in government," I told him. "But," I said, "we now have a new law for kids that might change foster care as we know it."

Duncan was right. I left. Still, a landmark law was passed. But I had to respect his caution. He didn't simply oppose change. He wanted to do our current work right, and he worried that the new work might not get done with integrity. Don't tell me that "bureaucrats" don't care.

7. Never Lose the Faces, the Stories

Perhaps it's lack of imagination on my part but policy alone doesn't move me. What happens to a person or a community *because of policy* does.

I am unable to accept a speaking engagement without also planning to visit a local program or a group. This is not to show how magnanimous I am as in, "Today's keynote speaker visited...." It is much more selfish. I learn. I am inspired. At a minimum, I have been given stories, faces, and flesh for policy and program. And some of those visits have changed policy. When I served as U.S. Commissioner of the Administration for Children Youth and Families in the late '70s, I would visit my ten regional offices across the nation, inevitably visiting local programs. I once attended a Head Start parents' meeting in a church basement. I wound up speaking with a mother who confided in me that her child was now a better reader than she, and that because of it, the mother had decided to enroll in school. When back in Washington, we changed an administrative regulation because of that mother, that face: all parents of Head Start children would have to volunteer, even if only an hour a week, and even if only spreading mayonnaise on bread. Subsequent studies showed the profound impact Head Start had on both children and parents.

Justice Resource Institute (JRI), a non-profit agency in Massachusetts I ran in the mid-1970s, launched the state's first pre-trial diversion programs. I recall speaking with one youth whose words stick with me to this day. He said, "Yes, I robbed her, but I had a lousy lawyer." I was stunned: admission of guilt, but denial of any human connectedness. The sole issue in the offender's mind was a legal one. Because of that short conversation I began an initiative called "Urban Court," which was, in essence, justice as reconciliation, in which offenders met their victims with community members as mediators (that is, if the victim and prosecuting attorney agreed). I wanted to embed the criminal act in a human context—to give a face to the victim and to the offender. The program attempted to convey two messages to youth: you are responsible, and you can make whole—help repair the damage, help heal the victim's pain. Most youth involved in the criminal justice system don't feel they have anything to give, anything of worth that anyone needs. In Urban Court, they showed they could. The results were stunning. Kids did "make whole." They got into trouble less. Subsequently, JRI received an Award of Recognition from then-U.S. Attorney General Griffin Bell. Urban Court became one of the progenitors of the restorative justice movement then beginning to gain traction across the country.

Perhaps it's the quirk in my memory, but some of the titles of the programs and policies with which I've been intimately involved are sometimes difficult to evoke, but the names and faces—10-year-old Tanika Riley in the Robert Taylor Homes in Chicago, Matty Lawson in Los Angeles, Bobby in Massachusetts, Kevin Grant in Oakland and so many more—seem to endure.

8. Consider Yourselves Fortunate

Whether you're running a program or serve in a policy position at the local, state or federal level, you are one of the lucky ones. There may be some sweaty moments in front of angry citizens, a dubious city council or legislative committee, a promising client who suddenly disappoints or a shrinking stream of funding. But how many people can say at the end of the day—or at the end of their days—"I protected a child and that child's life is better because of my work. The bullets have stopped flying. Our youth's life prospects are better. That neighborhood is safer and better. My city is better."

You can.

Most of you are driven by faith or a thirst for social justice or an unquenchable desire to relieve pain, or outrage about what is happening to those on society's margins. Realize that our work is a calling, not a career. In his book, *Passion for the Possible*, William Coffin states the difference brilliantly:

A career seeks to be successful, a calling to be valuable. A career tries to make money, a calling tries to make a difference... the words "car" and "career" come from "carrera," the Latin word for racetrack. This suggests that a car and a career both have you going in circles rapidly and competitively. Calling on the other hand, comes from the Latin "vocare," to call. A career demands technical intelligence to learn a skill, to find out how to get from here to there. A calling demands critical intelligence to question whether "there" is worth going toward.

What fuels our callings differs. What keeps us between despair and hope, wounds and healing, mistrust and trust, isolation, and connection, differs. However, what we do share is that fact that we're "called" to stand in the breach no matter what comes, a calling to which, in Chapter 58, Isaiah sums up beautifully:

Your ancient ruins shall be rebuilt;
They shall raise up the foundations of many generations;
You shall be called the repairer of the breach;
The restorer of the streets to dwell in.

It is a gift to be called. Consider yourself fortunate.

CHAPTER 14

Leadership

"For people to accept your leadership or want to engage with you, they've got to have some sense of who you are, what you believe, what's calling you. Martin Luther King Jr. didn't begin with 'I have a plan.' He began with 'I have a dream.'"

Books are written about leadership, usually not short sections of a book as are written here. However, I've served in the public arena for five decades, and, while I don't presume to write the final credo on the subject, some of the leadership lessons I've learned are important, if not essential, for those serving in leadership positions in the public sector. For me, these lessons stand the test of time, lessons learned by both successes and mistakes.

Put Vision at the Top of Your List

Not just what you're doing, but why. We human beings are meaning-seekers. We will do almost anything if we view a task as important, usually something bigger than ourselves, something that will help others, something replete with meaning.

Without a compelling vision, egos and turf protection take over. You are a persuader and a framer.

"Life is not primarily a quest for pleasure, as Freud believed, or a quest for power, as Alfred Adler taught, but a quest for meaning. The greatest task for any person is to find meaning in his or her life."

-Viktor Frankl, Man's Search for Meaning

That vision must be grounded in the needs of real people in real, hurting communities. It is through stories that a leader makes his or her values and responsibilities clear. For people to accept your leadership or want to engage with you, they've got to have some sense of who you are, what you believe, what's calling you. Martin Luther King Jr. didn't begin with "I have a plan." He began with, "I have a dream."

Learn. Constantly.

A leader is an animate sponge, a constant learner, one sensitive to trends, to research, to knowledge of effective practice, to evidence-based programs, and to the lives of others. The editorial writer Michael Gerson takes this one step further, citing the importance of empathy as, "the ability to identify with the emotions of others" (*Washington Post*, 6/1/2012, p. A 19). For Gerson, this seemingly squishy skill has critically important and hard applications, for the ability to identify with others "can inspire sacrifice" and "a commitment to justice." On some probably inarticulate level, I had an almost impossible time going for a few weeks without getting out of the office sharing thoughts with those whose lives we were trying to help, or whose pain we were trying to assuage. This was not paternalism, the leader mixing with the masses. Quite the reverse—people, youth, mothers, clinicians, whoever—were teaching me. "Public empathy," continues Gerson, "also expands the boundaries of a community. People in grief and need benefit from the assurance that their difficult journey is shared."

Translate Empathy into Action

The leader's next task is to translate that empathy into action. When people feel heard, that the leader has articulated their needs, framed appropriate responses, the leader will have partners. Leaders must communicate internally and externally. A leader must budget as much time as possible communicating with the widest possible variety of audiences. When I served as Commissioner of DYS in Massachusetts, I shared our mission, progress and challenges with every major editorial board in the state. I testified, as noted above. I was a frequent media guest and spoke at gatherings both small, such as an interfaith breakfast in the core city, and large, such as the state's annual Human Services Providers Forum. And I communicated with my staff through weekly staff meetings and periodic retreats. Such opportunities put me in arenas where I shared and was challenged, where I taught and learned. I've done the same in every major job I've held.

Identify Common Values:

Forge a Common Mission

Leadership can extend to those over whom you have zero authority. I helped to create the California Cities Violence Prevention Network under the aegis of the National League of Cities Institute for Youth, Education, and Families. I "ran" it for almost seven years. "Ran" is a poor verb. "Coordinated" maybe, but even that doesn't capture the shared commitment to the mission and to each other. Those committed to the Network reported to mayors, city managers, parks and recreation, or public health. Although I was their "leader," they were not my staff. We forged plans together; we held monthly phone calls, annual meetings and published both a newsletter and topical "papers." The subscription to the work and vision was so total that each city representative stood ready to journey to another city to help. Yes, vital information was shared, ("How did you get your school system to change that policy? Why did you put police officers in the youth center?"), policies were changed, but, at the root, they shared a similar mission, they cared deeply about each other, they were there for each other without question.   Tyrants feed on fear and disintegration.   In contrast, a good leader helps identify common values, and helps to forge a common mission based on those values.

Build Two Roofs Over the Heads of Your Staff

One has to do with meaning, with vision, the importance of the work. Staff have got to come to work knowing they're doing something important.   The other has to do with clarity of expectation, where they're going, and supporting the work both financially and personally and by minimizing surprises. You need to provide an optimal context in which work can get done. Some label the dual thrusts mission and means to achieve the mission.

It should be noted that these two elements—the mission, the inspiration and the requisite systems—aren't always in harmony. And they shouldn't be. A dynamic tension should exist. A secular and theological metaphor might serve well here. Many non-profits or even units of government began small, "in garages" if you will. They were mission-driven, exciting, entrepreneurial. Roles and authority were often unclear. Metaphorically speaking, who handled the wrench or who was under the car or who did the wiring could vary from day to day. With success came growth and requisite systems to support the growth. But was the initial vision retained or did maintenance become the sole goal? The same can be expressed theologically as well. After inspirational starts, temples and churches were built, liturgies created, rites perfected, priest-craft honed. But then the prophets would storm in excoriating the leaders, telling them that they had forgotten why they had built the temples and that they were now worshipping structure, abandoning their initial mission, which was and is to feed the hungry, heal the sick, visit the lonely.

A healthy agency will continue to refresh itself, confronting bravely the inherent tension between the original vision and current practice. It's a paradox: a healthy agency will create a built-in tension between the priestly and the prophetic. Create a learning community where ideas are welcomed and renewal is built into the way you lead your agency.

Get Out of Your Staff's Way

After inspiring and trying to provide some clarity about roles and how things fit, get out of your staff's way. Give them room for creativity and autonomy. Let them own something. Celebrate their successes. Be bountiful with your thanks. And remember that sharing ownership means sharing the burden. Your shoulders may be broad, but you are human. You can't do it all and shouldn't. Let your staff thrive and shine.

Treat Staff with Kindness and Respect and Expect the Best

Meghan Biro writing about leadership in *Forbes* magazine notes that "nice leaders don't finish last. They finish first, again and again. Ignorance and arrogance are leadership killers...treating everyone with a basic level of respect is an absolute must trait of leadership. And kindness is the gift that keeps on giving back." She notes, of course, that those who don't deserve such kindness and respect "must be dealt with." Equally important, look for and appreciate the good in your staff.

Set the bar high. Push staff to a higher plane, loftier goals, which, in turn makes staff feel very good when they achieve some of these goals. Be unrelenting about quality and generous with praise. Work as hard or harder than your most hard-working staff. Hold yourself and your staff accountable. And listen, listen, listen.

Conventional leadership wisdom asks followers to believe in leaders. But the real question is whether leaders believe in "followers," conveying to staff that they can be effective, that lofty goals can be reached. Leader belief in followers manifests itself in many ways— sharing power, investing in training, removing barriers, providing clarity, dealing with conflict. Leaders lose their staff when followers withdraw their consent to be led.

Be Honest

Staff, your funders, your board, your bosses need clarity, not BS. A crisis can make or break a leader. Learn from a crisis. Don't hide your problems because they will return, next time in larger form. Machiavelli preyed on and based his theory of government on fear and mistrust. Your job is the opposite: build trust. If you're not honest about what's going on, your staff will then only value self-protection and preservation, not honesty. And you will give rise to those who would undercut the work. Face reality, starting with yourself. Create safe spaces where staff can be vulnerable and honest. Apologizing must not be viewed as beneath a leader. Someone once said "never waste a good crisis." A crisis can expose a weakness. Confront it candidly. Use it to build, rather than separate, your team. Emerge from a crisis stronger, more confident about the future.

Don't Terminate People the Way I Did

Although impelled by a moral force or the stories of those who inspire the work, sensible, well-run programs must be shaped. One doesn't help those in need if the necessary business aspects of the work aren't well attended to. In 1983 I helped to found and become the first President and CEO of the National Crime Prevention Council (NCPC) whose mission it was to help stop crime and build vital communities that don't produce crime. We were able to raise funds from public and private sources, launch new and innovative programs, and watch our staff grow from four at our start to 83.

After almost 20 years of steady growth, things slowed and I faced my first ever need to cut staff. It's tough enough to lay off staff. It is tougher to lay off those you've hired, and I had hired almost all of NCPC's employees. When I was running a large government agency under President Carter, I had a staff of more than 4,000 and a budget close to $1B. If layoffs or transfers occurred, someone else did the dirty work. On one level, I believe strongly that running a modest-sized non-profit is more difficult than managing a large federal agency, in part because of the intimacy and camaraderie. We felt we were on the vanguard of redefining crime prevention from protection of property and surveillance to building community health and supporting youth development. And to a degree we were. Staff retention was extremely high, our mission shared, and the work climate healthy. It was a vital place, a place of innovation, of program and policy rigor and fun.

That is until I faced laying off my first staff. I first cut executive salaries, and then formed an agency-wide task force to help me determine criteria for staff retention/removal. This was a mistake—a big one. Contention rather than cooperation characterized the task force meetings. People stopped sharing, rather, they began to protect their turf, this counter to the sharing ethos that had characterized the agency for almost two decades. Backbiting began as some staff sought to elevate themselves at the expense of others. Staff were scared, their livelihoods threatened. The process dragged on. Morale and the work climate, for the first time, suffered. One of the prime jobs of a leader is to provide a roof, to create a healthy work environment in which good, creative work gets done. During this time, NCPC's work climate was not healthy.

Somehow we stumbled through it, finally having to lay off about five staff. We got back on our feet, but there were wounds, some of which persisted.

Were I to do it again, I'd be extremely clear up front with board and staff about criteria for layoffs. Craft and adopt a policy with your board and follow it. When faced with layoffs, I'd act quickly and transparently. I'd offer to write letters of recommendation for departing staff who would leave with honor and support, and, if they were up for it, a party.

Excepting the last few years as a consultant, I have led a variety of agencies. After working in youth and community development through Boston's poverty program, Action for Boston Community Development, I helped to found and run Justice Resource Institute. Subsequently, Governor Dukakis asked me to serve as his State Commissioner of the Department of Youth Services. President Carter appointed me to the post of Commissioner of the Administration for Children, Youth and Families, then, after a short stint as Vice President of the Child Welfare League of America, it was on to NCPC. You'd think I would have been prepared for this most awful of tasks. But with all the community work I've done, the program and policy shaping, the testifying before city councils, state legislatures and Congress, the management of agencies large and small, and the keynotes here and abroad, nothing, nothing was more difficult for me than laying off staff.

Don't Shoot the Messenger

Immediately following my job as Commissioner of AYCF, I was hired to serve as Vice President of the Child Welfare League of America (CWLA). I didn't last long. By definition a national organization such as CWLA exists in constant tension between the needs in the field and the need to pay attention to national policy. I shouldered a good bit of the field work, presented all over the nation and returned with baggage full of information, much of it unpleasant. I suggested ways of solving problems, changes in policy and practice, throughout indicating that the League, while based on a time-honored mission was in danger of losing members, which indeed it was. Members were refusing to pay dues, dropping out. I loved CWLA and its mission, but it was hurting and I was not quiet. Within a short time, I think less than a year, it became pretty clear that this was not a heaven-forged match. It was not long before a mutually agreed upon divorce was being drafted. Soon after I left, the board fired the director. Subsequently the board, along with the headhunter, came to me offering me the job. As the National Crime Prevention Council was just beginning to take shape, I made what was a very tough decision for me: I refused the offer. The point here: don't shoot the messenger, you may offer him another job someday. Note: CWLA has been in very good hands since.

Nurture Truly Vital Partnerships

As a leader, a big part of your job is to bring partners to the table and to get them excited about being there. Most successful endeavors aren't based on solo flying. Case in point, vital partnerships lie at the heart of the California Cities Violence Prevention Network and the National Forum on Youth Violence Prevention. "Vital" is the key word, as in having vitality, a pulse, a drive, a passion. At worst, partnerships involve a variety of agencies meeting dutifully (sometimes under duress) with representatives whose arms are folded and who have no intention of changing how they do business. They are as unyielding as Lego blocks, like a marriage on auto pilot—no real communication, no real change.

As Mario Maciel pointed out in Chapter 11, it is the leader's role to know his or her partners, to know and respect their missions, and to show how a partner's mandate might fit into the whole. The July-August 1992 issue of the *Harvard Business Review* cites an ancient Chinese parable about the wheel:

"Never forget that a wheel is made not only of spokes but also of the space between the spokes. Sturdy spokes poorly placed make a weak wheel. Whether their full potential is realized depends on the harmony between them. The essence of wheel making lies in the craftsman's ability to conceive and create the space that holds and balances the spokes within the wheel."

The leader's job is to help make partner boundaries porous, to break or at least crack silos, to spur partners to rethink how they're doing what they're doing and how modest changes in practice can improve the whole. This takes the creation of and partner subscription to a larger vision while acknowledging and honoring the individual mandate of each partner. Again, as we see in the California Cities Violence Prevention Network example, the creation and implementation of a city's comprehensive plan catalyzed changes in how city and county agencies do business—police patrolling with the faith community, probation officers assigned to schools, police serving as mentors, hospitals launching hospital-bed violence reduction programs, schools totally rethinking suspension policies, the business community providing pro bono management advice, separate agencies sharing data, and so much more.

Stoke Your Energy

Your job is to elicit and provide energy. You're one of the main sources of passion. But we're human. Stamina and energy wane, so take care of yourself. What works for me is being with my children and grandkids, an evening (of course with wine) with friends, tending my garden, playing tennis and travel. Music nourishes me. I sing in a local choir. Just sing. I don't run it, manage it or raise funds for it. Just sit in my chair and sing. Find your song outside of your work and sing it.

Know the Real Source of Your Authority

You should be very clear about the source of your authority. Yes, it may seem to be a governor or a president or a statute or a mayor or a city council or a board, but it's deeper than that. Much deeper. Your real authority doesn't stem from your uniform, your title, or your position. No: Your real power is intrinsic, not extrinsic. Ultimately, you are authorized and commissioned by the child who needs you, the family in disarray, those about to be victimized, those about to victimize, kids who need to attend school without fear, and those who are disconnected from family, neighborhood, school and hope.

And Finally, Go Where the Fire Is

We are challenged to work in four concentric but interconnected circles—self, family, neighborhood and the larger community. What can I do myself? What can I do to change the context, change policies? Under it all are passion, commitment and risk—deeper principles.

Recall the movie, *Gandhi*. India in the 1940s fought and gained independence from England. But the Indian subcontinent split violently into Hindu and Muslim factions. As the separate states of India and Pakistan formed, fighting, looting and murder became rampant.

A summit meeting was held in the ornate Governor's Palace in New Delhi. The British, Hindu, and Muslim leaders attended. The negotiations were intense. Suddenly Gandhi with his tiny bag of possessions got up and started to walk out. "Where are you going? You cannot leave us. Stay," begged the leaders. Said Gandhi, "I am going to Calcutta: that's where the fire is."

Be where the fire is. Or be the fire. Life is too short, the fires many. And be grateful that you have such passion. And yes, you will get burned, but fired up, you never will have lived so well—or walked such a magnificent journey.

Testifying: The Art of Sharing Your Mission with Supporters and Skeptics

Testifying before city councils, state legislatures or Congress should not be viewed as an invitation to an inquisition, but as an opportunity to tell your story. Legislators enact a law or allocate public funds for an activity or for the implementation of a statute. You are the steward of these funds and the implementer of a statute they may have passed. You're the temporary steward; they are the owners. Your job: make them proud of what they created. Remember, it's not about you: it's about those whose lives have been changed because of what they have set in motion.

Your auditors should see you as someone who knows what you're talking about. If you're asking for more funding, you should anchor your request in the agency's mission—the statute you were pledged to honor, the program you were asked to administer— and you should embody what you're trying to do in a story. Make it real. Give it flesh. Then and only then get into the numbers or the details of your request or your report. Be brutally honest about implementation issues or problems with the statute itself. If there are problems, underscore your proposed solutions, and follow up. "This is something we've been wrestling with for three months. We're getting help from the state's attorney. We'd like to schedule another hearing before you in eight weeks to report on progress—and hopefully a solution to this problem." Take the initiative, take action or they will. Always assume they are interested even though many look catatonic or bored as they work through a long line of witnesses.

Try to avoid surprises by meeting with legislative staff beforehand. Find out what most concerns or excites the subcommittee or council. If needed, bring in a constituent or two, those who have benefitted from the work, referring to them in your testimony, indicating that they are present in the audience.

As noted, the Justice Resource Institute launched the first pre-trial diversion programs in Massachusetts. Diversion rested on the discretion of a prosecutor or a judge. A youth would be diverted to us for a minor offense, and if that youth did well—secured a job, returned to school, completed drug abuse counseling— charges were dismissed. Who was diverted and why varied wildly throughout the courts in which we worked. We felt diversion should be more formalized, and so we went about the task of drafting a new law. We worked closely with staff of key state legislators on the Justice Subcommittee. We secured the political backing of the more conservative community – police, judges and prosecutors. When we presented the law, testified on it, the work had, in point of fact, been done. The hearings, largely cosmetic, were a breeze. The Massachusetts State Legislature passed the nation's first pre-trial diversion laws.

Sounds good? Yes. But also know you will be surprised.

Things differed when I first took over at the Massachusetts DYS, an agency beset by controversy, an agency in chaos, and agency frequently targeted by angry state legislators. My most significant initial achievement was getting a year's grace from the legislature, a year in which the state's task force on juvenile corrections, which I had established with the attorney general, would report, a year for my agency to put in place desperately needed systems, a year to even find some of the youth committed to us. A year. Otherwise the legislature pledged to reopen the massive, inhumane "training schools" it had shuttered. The upshot: I stayed close to the legislature and to legislative staff, reporting on progress and difficulties. There was trust. Legislators knew I cared about kids AND public safety. Eventually a sound, responsive system was created, and the training schools stayed closed.

However, two surprises occurred. One happened during my second or third year testifying on my budget. I testified with my boss, Jerry Stevens, he of the dazzling chart, who sat so close to me that our shoulders almost touched. I think I worried him, so he stayed close. At one point, Chairman Finnegan asked me whether the committee's proposed budget cuts would have a negative effect on the work at DYS. "Yes," I blurted out, "it will hurt my agency terribly. We're making progress and need every cent we can get," I recall saying. I also recall a very well-directed heel painfully squashing my big toe. (Funny how I recall his feet. They were unusually narrow: narrow and pointed.) I looked at him, startled, his heel increasing the pressure, his face now about a foot away, his eyes looking like a compactor ready to crush and dispense with me. Commissioners were supposed to go along with the administration's numbers. In the heat of the discussion, I went with my agency's need, not the pre-agreed upon numbers. Jerry took me to the woodshed. But legislature gave me my budget.

Then I was jumped. I think I had emerged both as an effective change agent and system builder. I wanted to be held accountable, and was. My progressive credentials, I thought, were impeccable: After all, I had taught in the slums, worked with youth in Boston's core city where I had also done community development, and I had pioneered diversion and restitution programs. And so, when the most liberal of state senators, Jack Backman from Brookline summoned me to a hearing, I thought I'd be sharing with a soul mate. Not so.

Part of my work as DYS Commissioner involved closing community programs that didn't make sense, that weren't working, that were even hurting kids. There weren't many, but there were some, and they were egregiously awful. At the same time I was opening small, secure locked settings for the state's most violent. I wanted the horrible state training schools to remain closed, but I had to do something about security. It was a moral issue: I wanted these kids in my system, not in the adult system to which many of the judges were sending them because of the absence of security in DYS.

I entered the hearing room only to find representatives from a few of the community programs we had closed ready to testify against DYS. Against! The conservatives had slammed DYS for not attending to security, and here were the liberals slamming DYS for "abandoning" the community-based movement. Nothing could have been further from the truth.
I felt unjustly accused, personally insulted, and completely misunderstood. I had taken the DYS job specifically to create a viable community-based system from what was a nascent community-based movement. I felt this public excoriation would erode our progress to date and drain our political capital. Somehow my two deputies and I endured a 60-minute string (maybe it was only 20) of unrelenting accusations. Our staff held

together. The mission stayed intact. We periodically briefed—
but never seemed to make happy—Senator Backman's staff.

President Carter nominated me to serve as his Chief of the
Children's Bureau (aka The Administration for Children, Youth and
Families). I had come down from Massachusetts, working for
ACYF as Acting Commissioner while preparing for my hearing. I
ran the agency but had no signatory authority. To prepare for my
nomination hearing, I was briefed daily, and I studied at night.

When the date for my hearing arrived, I felt like an athlete ready
to go. I brought a stack of briefing books and statutes to the
witness stand. My deputies and other staff sat in the public area.
After my opening statement, which proudly described ACYF's
history and a brief picture of our promising future, I awaited
questions. There was a long pause before Senator Long from
Louisiana asked with a slow drawl, "Son, you any kin to John C.
Calhoun?" This was the first question? I responded in the
affirmative. He followed up. "Son, after the hearing I'd like you
to see my desk. It was John C's, the one he used as Vice
President." Of course I'd be delighted to come to his office. Was
that really the first question about ACYF's precious mandate,
about America's children? The second question concerned
something about interstate custody laws related to divorce about
which I had no idea. I think Senator Wallop from Wyoming asked
the question. Of course I'd get back to the committee—next
week. Another long pause ensued. We were about five minutes
into the hearing. The chairman looked to his left, then right, then
raised the gavel, asked for a vote, got it, and I was voted in,
approved in the space of about five minutes. Stunned, I didn't
leave the stand. As they shuffled papers preparing for the next

nominee, I said something like, "I'd be delighted to answer additional questions about ACYF's mandate and more detail about our plans for the future." I was an athlete on the field! I hadn't been tested. I wanted to be tested. The senators looked at me curiously. My hearing had ended. I was told politely that there would be ample time for more in-depth discussions in the future, that I was now Commissioner and that they had other presidential nominations to consider.

In other words, leave. I joined Senator Long in his office; he proudly showing me the nicks and scratches on John C's desk, I barely holding my tongue about John C's repugnant views on slavery.

A note about proactive testimonies: After helping to design the California Cities Gang Prevention Network (CCGPN—later the California Cities Violence Prevention Network) in 2006, I set about "selling" it to cities and city councils up and down the state of California. CCGPN represented the vanguard, the new way of reducing violence and building community. At each hearing, I was asked about funding. There was none, I told the city counselors. But I promised this: a reduction in violent crime; changes in the quality of life; the creation of something new and promising, changes in policy and the attraction of additional resources. City Councils actually seemed excited about being on the vanguard. Every city, eventually thirteen of them, signed on.

Almost all of the thirteen cities that had signed on forged comprehensive plans blending prevention, intervention, enforcement and reentry. I believe additional funding came to every city, and it came from a variety of sources—local, state, federal, and philanthropic. It came because funders saw their funding for a specific program not alone, but now in a robust context, in the context of a citywide commitment in which their funds could be leveraged and even sustained.

And policy did change. Two state laws were altered, and, of greater importance, the U.S. Department of Justice adopted the California model in 2010, calling it The National Forum on Youth Violence Prevention, as of this writing in 15 cities across America.

View testimonies as marvelous opportunities to tell your story, advocate for a social change agenda, gain allies, change social policy, and give people hope. Seek these opportunities. Help create them. Realize though, like fuel, they can be volatile, and should be handled with care.

CHAPTER 15

Engaging the Philanthropic and Business Communities as Partners

"...the private sector...can move relatively swiftly, and...
take risks the government cannot or will not."

Without the philanthropic community, my policy walk would have been half as successful and half as fulfilling. Unlike government, philanthropies are flexible, can move quickly and, if philanthropic supporters are community foundations or a local business, the issues presented to them are not theoretical, but pressing—those they read about daily. Even when running a state agency—The Massachusetts Department of Youth Services—I could not have accomplished what I did without the private sector. I had to retrain workers when we "de-institutionalized" a large, locked system. DYS did not have the money for retraining. I set up a non-profit entity connected to DYS. The private sector funded it. Workers were retrained as community quality control agents. They liked their jobs better, as they too, were released from institutions, and a huge controversy that threatened to torpedo the deinstitutionalization movement—hundreds of state workers protesting the imminent loss of their jobs—was averted.

POLICY

The business and philanthropic sectors are integral parts of every community. Ideally "integral parts" not peripheral parts, as the well-being of this sector is intimately connected to community health and well-being. Business will not invest in communities torn apart by crime. Loans to small businesses, an essential part of every community and to individuals who need support for a house or car, shrink or dry up altogether in violent neighborhoods. Schools fail to train workers that businesses need. Citizen buying power atrophies.

When families fray, schools fail to educate, and the economy cannot produce jobs, crime often rises. Typically, society turns to law enforcement to keep the social fabric from deteriorating further. This places an unfair and impossible burden on law enforcement, and it fails to hold all of us accountable.

Crime and fear of crime create isolation, inhibiting communities from developing appropriately. Our response to the fragmentation caused by crime is often equally fragmented—a program here, a program there to stanch the wounds. As noted in Chapter 11, "Comprehensive Strategies," what's needed is a comprehensive response that harnesses and focuses the energies of all community entities – local government, schools, law enforcement, public health, the faith community and the business and philanthropic communities, to name a few. When communities deteriorate, businesses deteriorate or they move out. "Crime affects us all. What affects the city, affects us," asserts Victoria Dinges, Allstate's Vice President for Corporate Social Responsibility. Allstate pledged to raise $50m for crime and violence prevention because, says Dinges, "for Chicago to become a global city and economic powerhouse such as Los Angeles and New York, it has to deal with Chicago's crime problem."

Few foundations fund violence prevention efforts directly. Most support education, the arts, mentoring, jobs programs and the like. Yet crime and violence erode private sector investments in these areas. If kids are afraid to attend school, no amount of investment in quality education will help unless chronic absenteeism is curbed and dropping out reduced. "We fund health, education, family economic success, but no matter our route in, we kept running into the youth violence issue," said Sharnita Johnson, Project Officer at the Kellogg Foundation. "The core reason [we invest in violence prevention] has to do with pervasive fear in the community, fear that meant we couldn't fully realize our investments in other areas," echoes Paul Grogan, President of the Boston Foundation. This doesn't mean that foundations have to alter their core purpose, but it does mean that their investments should be coordinated with others, so that the investments of each, public and private, can be maximized.

Finally, utilitarian arguments, such as economic ones, pale in comparison to the moral imperative: too many kids are dying. Violence has hollowed out too many communities. Said Sylvia Zaldivar-Sykes of the Lake County Community Foundation, "We couldn't ignore that our number one civil right, safety, is an elusive right for too many of our youth…we cannot ignore the injustice of living in a persistently violent neighborhood."

Given funding streams, requests for proposals and legal and policy strictures the government, typically, is slow to react. Conversely, the private sector, not so bound, can move relatively swiftly, and it can take risks the government cannot or will not. "Who else would fund a grandmother to run an afterschool program where no one plays in the streets or rides a bike?" asks Sykes, who reports that crime has dropped and that kids are again playing in the street.

WALKING

Some foundations have pooled resources to accomplish a major objective well beyond the reach of a single donor. In Pittsburgh, 20 foundations of varying sizes such as Heinz, BNY Mellon, Buhl, and Alcoa joined forces to build a massive and complex data sharing structure, ("Data Warehouse"), between the Department of Human Services (Mental Health, Homeless Services, Family Support, Child

Welfare and more), and participating school systems all with the intent of sharing data so that those in need could be better know and better served. (For more on data sharing see Chapter 12.)

Boston's State Street Foundation with the Boston Foundation has created the Youth Violence Prevention Funders Learning Collaborative (YVPFLC). "We bring together private and public sector funders, experts and stakeholders to learn, share, and act in order to align funding to address gaps and barriers that prevent youth violence in neighborhoods in Boston where 80 percent of the violent crime occurs," says Sheila Peterson, Vice President of Corporate Citizenship at State Street Bank. Key YVPFLC funding strategy areas include: Workforce Development and Education, Youth Development and Mentoring, and Family Supports and Mental Health. The Stoneleigh Foundation has helped to pull together a similar collaborative in Philadelphia.

Don't Dismiss Passion and Compassion: Julio Marcial, The California Wellness Foundation

Foundations have mission statements. They set priories, issue guidelines, review proposals, and either fund or not. Sometimes it's difficult to find the passion under the mission, the animating beliefs under priorities and guidelines.

Some foundation officers begin with policy—a few with searing personal experience. Julio Marcial's formal title—Project Director at the California Wellness Foundation—does little to convey the passion and commitment Marcial brings to his work—and the reasons for his passion.

California Wellness' mission "is to improve the health of the people of California by making grants for health promotion, wellness education and disease prevention." Its goals include:

- To address the particular health needs of traditionally underserved populations, including low-income individuals, people of color, youth, and residents of rural areas;
- To support and strengthen nonprofit organizations that seek to improve the health of underserved populations;
- To recognize and encourage leaders who are working to increase health and wellness within their communities; and
- To inform policymakers and opinion leaders about important wellness and health care issues.

There is a difference between the formally stated mission and goals, and speaking with a foundation staffer who embodies them.

Marcial grew up in a zip code where, "violence was the norm along with pawn shops, junk yards and crime." His father, who was undocumented, took whatever job he could, "all under the radar— cook, janitor, gardener, whatever. He always told me," says Marcial, "do something you love, not what you have to." And he is. "I love this work, the foundation work. It is a privilege. I get paid to fight for justice?" he asks incredulously. "I can't believe it."

The first in his family to attend college, he studied the overrepresentation of black and brown youth in the juvenile justice system while at USC Santa Barbara. Just after graduation in July 1998, he got a job ("Boy, was I lucky.") in communications at the California Wellness Foundation. Wellness, with a small handful of foundations from across the nation, helped to shift policy tectonic plates, namely helping move violence from a criminal justice to a public health issue. "You see it can be prevented. We know the reasons, and we know why, like pathogens, violence spreads."

He is as comfortable on the streets, in jails, in violence-torn schools as he is in the office making funding decisions: One might argue, more comfortable. "This is how I learn," he says vehemently. "I get as close as possible to see, touch, hear, walk with. If nothing else it stokes my indignation, reminds me why I'm doing this work."

To Marcial, the work is messy, "as it should be because these are messy problems. If you're looking for comfort," he advises, "don't get into this work because if you do it right, you're going to be uncomfortable, wonderfully uncomfortable," he adds. He feels that "boxes and arrows and logic models" can often shield us from what's really going on, from "hard, messy truths."

Engagement gives Marcial the faces, the fuel to keep going, and a picture of policy issues painted not by studies, but by youth on the street, kids in school, youth in jail. "We can't turn a blind eye to the widening income gap, poor education and no jobs," he says. Wellness has been "hammering at it for more than 20 years." The faces make the policy issues come to life—painfully so.

His philosophy of grant making rests, it seems, on two pillars: funding projects that focus on outcomes, and funding "advocacy to help change unjust structures. Therefore," he continues, "it gets messy in both areas—program implementation in tough situations, and tough policy discussions on the county, state and federal levels."

He feels that foundations must "embrace the complexity," and not always follow algorithms, but "take risks, embrace rigor and complexity." He feels that with two decades of "feats and defeats" at Wellness that they are best when they serve as a "marketplace of ideas." Learning is constant, even in defeat, he maintains. "We just lost on the Juvenile Solitary Confinement issue. But guess what? We've never had so many allies, and they'll be with us for the next battle. We'll be stronger." He cites Wellness Foundation's work on the gun issue as another example. "We were hit with veto after veto year after year until now where we have the most stringent gun bills in the nation." He also points to the recently passed Prop 47, which permits the early release of offenders serving time in jail for certain offenses. Framing for the Proposition's successes: "Equip these guys to be good, contributing citizens so that they don't cause more trouble when they come home," he notes.

He reflects on the past when it was "pretty lonely, and there were not many of us," to today where "there are millions in back of this work, and public health departments from across the nation are viewing the violence as a public health issue—and they are acting on it."

"And you've got to give policy makers stories," Marcial maintains. "They have short attention spans. Get them close, close to a kid, someone working two jobs trying to keep a family together, a youth shot on the way to school."

What keeps him going? "I stand on the shoulders of the trailblazers to whom I have an obligation to carry on the work. Until someone tells me to stop being in the mess, seeing pain, inspired by hope, I'll continue. Personally," he says, "I'm a work in progress. It's a marathon. It never gets easier. But it gets better because there are more of us, and I get to experience hope first hand."

Gang Reduction Youth Development (GRYD) zones have been set up in the most violent neighborhoods in Los Angeles. GRYD funding requires key neighborhood entities, the police, schools, zoning, the faith community, public health, and others to focus and coordinate their collective efforts on reducing violence and building healthy neighborhoods. One of the GRYD zones is located in the neighborhood where Julio grew up. "There's less violent crime. More neighborhood participation, and a sprinkling of businesses. It IS messy. The work IS constant, but I also see hope all around me. Now seeing that, how could I ever stop this work? I'm blessed."

Working with the Private Sector

Do your homework about what a particular foundation or business has funded. But don't be trapped by it. Start always with your vision, your passion and, wherever possible, illustrate your idea with a face, a story. Be very clear about what the outcome will look like and how you will measure success. Then listen and listen well. And don't give up: foundation guidelines seem always in flux. And do not look at the private sector as a cash cow, for there are many ways they can help (see below). View them as a partner, someone co-creating the work with you, joining forces to tackle a pressing social problem. One might get lucky and receive a grant. Don't start there. Understand what worries them. Find their passion, the Julio Marcial in them. Let them know they are not alone, that their investment, whatever it may be, will be leveraged because it is part of a larger, comprehensive effort.

The Many Ways the Private Sector Can Participate

- Research: Successful businesses have significant research, analytic/tracking capacities. Crime trends, hot spots and measurement are essential parts of violence prevention work.
- Convening: Typically, the business and philanthropic sectors can bring together influential players.
- Capacity Building: These sectors know how to train and build capacity. Ask them for help. If nothing else, ask them for space for your training (you might get a meal, too).
- Policy Support: Involve them in your citywide violence prevention governance structure. Also, private sector testimony before city councils or state legislators is not only a surprise (not your usual advocate) but is usually from someone credible and well known.
- Supporting Conferences: Most in the violence prevention field hold local or state conferences. Private support for these gatherings is not difficult when free publicity is given to the sponsor.
- Claim their Hearts: The security company ADT made significant contributions to the National Crime Prevention

Council over a 15-year period. The contributions went well beyond a check. ADT funded a series of "Local Heroes in Crime Prevention" awards throughout the nation with each local office sponsoring an awards ceremony. "Not only did sales go up," reported then CEO Les Bruhaldi, "but staff morale shot up and staff retention soared. They loved doing it."

- And yes, Funding. The opportunities abound and can be tailored to the interests of the private sector. These are but a few of many examples:
  - Prevention: family support; beautification; recreation; pre-school education.
  - Intervention: mentoring; restorative justice; neighborhood patrols; job training.
  - Enforcement: Violence Interrupters; hot spot policing; citizen/police academies; Police Athletic League.
  - Reentry: mentoring; in-prison work; job training/provision; housing.

RESOURCES

- The Council on Foundations (http://www.councilonfoundations.org)
- The Chronicle of Philanthropy (http://philanthropy.com)
- Foundation Center (http://www.foundationcenter.org)

CHAPTER 16

Glossary of the Walk:

The Words that Keep Us on the Path

Public policy does not get us up in the morning: our core beliefs do, words and principles we do not always articulate, but which nonetheless motivate us to be our finest. We should be unafraid to bring to light the words that quicken and move us.

I've spent the bulk of my life helping to design and run programs in the public policy arena. I know that success requires certain policies and practices. We need the best and most robust of these. But policy may not capture the essence.

Policies don't explain Matty Lawson, who lost two of her children to gang violence. As a father of two, I cannot imagine a more horrible pain. But Matty was not destroyed by her staggering grief. Instead she turned to action, saying, "I no longer have two children, I have four hundred. Not one more child in my neighborhood will die."

I began my work probably by accident, having been swept up in the Civil Rights Movement by, Martin Luther King Jr. almost 50 years ago. I believe that if King had begun with policy, he would have failed. The changes that stream from his work dazzle: Head Start, Job Corps, and such monumental laws as the Voting Rights and Civil Rights Acts.

But he didn't begin there. He began with a passionate moral commitment. His framing was Exodus—escape from slavery, wandering in the desert, a view of the Promised Land, a dream of equality. Unheard of. Madness; perhaps holy madness. But the story found itself in every living room and every heart. He galvanized a nation: everyone who has lived has experienced some injustice, some pain, some desert. The story of Exodus brought us all in.

So while we hold the language of policy as precious, we must be unafraid of another glossary, perhaps the oldest, lurking just beneath the surface. Words like:

CLAIM

I was privileged to sit on United States Attorney General Janet Reno's Coordinating Council on Juvenile Justice. At one of our meetings held in the community, one presenter, a minister described what his church was doing. He mentioned Head Start, mentoring, family counseling, and after-school programs. He concluded: "We also go out on the streets and simply get to know the kids by name." He said this casually, at the end of his presentation. I was stunned. How wonderful, how powerful, for underneath the bravado of many kids, we find the ache, the loneliness, the pain of not being claimed, not being loved by anyone.

The message of claim, of knowing who a person is, goes both ways: it means that I care about you and will do everything in my power to help you. But it also means that I care about others in the community and will not let you harm an individual, a school, a neighborhood. As parents, we will neither let our children hurt others or be hurt. In this way, we are claiming both the health of the individual and the health of the community.

LONELINESS

I think too many of America's kids are colossally lonely. One might argue that the Columbine and Newtown murders were motivated by a hollow, primordial pain against those they perceived had rejected them. They murdered the source of their pain, their perceived exclusion. This does not in the least excuse their horrible acts, but it may help explain them. Legitimately, schools have tightened school policies following reports of school shootings, many of these policies have to do with exits and entrances, cameras, emergency procedures and responsibilities for key actors—administrators, teachers, parents, police and kids. All necessary, but what if our goal were a caring school? What would the school look and feel like if students felt more connected to each other and to caring adults? Would it mean a smaller or more intimate school? Schools within schools? What if we committed ourselves to a dense network of caring—big buddies, little buddies? Every child mentored, every child made responsible for another?

TRANSFORMATION

At its simplest, transformation means change. Here, it means risking change by being fully with another person. It is much safer, much easier to be distant with those with whom we work. Transformation is risky: it means we are in it together, and that I might be changed. Without risk, there is no change. This applies to individuals and to the various "silos" in which we work. Coming to the table as a representative of your "silo" is something, but not enough. Collective effort to address a specific issue such as community violence means a willingness to be open, to do business in a different way such as police volunteering to mentor tough kids, schools changing expulsion policies, prosecutors launching family counseling programs, courts sponsoring teen courts, and hospitals starting bedside reconciling programs.

RECONCILIATION

Communities have shown that they can take more responsibility for preventing crime. Teens have demonstrated that they can take more responsibility. The victimizer can also be held responsible for his or her actions especially in the context of restorative justice or sentencing circles. Without a context of reconciliation, there is no healing, no restoration. "Welcome Home" is the name of one program for offenders returning from jail. The capacity and obligation to make whole, to reweave the community fabric torn by crime, means that as the victimizer is responsible for attempting to reconcile with the community, so the community must reconcile with the victimizer.

STAY

Ours is a pretty atomized, overly busy world with people bumping into each other, talking to someone else on cell phones over lunch, too busy to chat, to engage. It's an impermanent world. Social services are generally episodic: a counselor, a probation officer, a social worker comes and goes, depending on the need. But who stays? Why not say, "I am here. I will not leave you." Pastor Eugene Rivers, a central figure in the "Boston Miracle" (plummeting crime rates in the mid-1990s) expressed the challenge this way, "The drug dealer is available 24/7, rain or shine, always there. We tend to go home at 5:00."

FREEDOM

Many with whom I've had the good fortune to work, especially those working on the streets in some of the toughest situations, believe deeply that they are not carrying the burden alone, and that they don't have to be perfect. Many spoke of the serenity and a diminished need to control. Most derived both power and meaning, not from an appointed or political office, but from the people they felt fortunate to serve. Many spoke of the grace, inspiration, and courage exhibited by those they served. Thus there was a correlation between their sense of the true source of power and a feeling of freedom. Most spiritual traditions say, "Be not afraid." They don't say we cannot have fear, because we all have fear. But they can say we do not have to BE our fears, and we do not have to create a world based on our fears.

CHAPTER 17

Pain Must Not Be Wasted

"...we the wounded healers, helping to heal the unhealed
wounders."

This chapter doesn't quite qualify as policy walking, more what's
under policy that keeps us walking, or if we're hobbling, what gives
meaning to the limp, strength to the step, however halting.

All But My Life

I met Gerda Weissmann Klein at the White House Conference on
Teenagers in May 2000. We sat next to each other in an afternoon
breakout session on the Youth as Resources session. We spoke briefly
about how we happened to be at this conference where we spoke of
the human spirit and of our shared mission—to recognize the resilient
spirit in youth, to claim it and nurture it, and to encourage
communities to use and celebrate it, to view youth as potential
resources, partners, not as hunks of pathology waiting to explode.

At the end of the session, she gave me an autographed copy of her
book, *All But My Life*. I didn't know she was a Holocaust survivor,
that her book is required reading in many schools across the nation,
and that a documentary based on her story had won an Academy
Award. What I did know, after reading her book, was that the heart
of this short, 76-year-old, passionate woman could have embraced a

city full of children. Two months later, Gerda who was busy with speaking engagements around the world, called my assistant to ask if I ever get out to Phoenix. I had traveled to Phoenix twice in 10 years. Fate intervened: I was leaving in two days to speak at a conference in Arizona.

Gerda invited me to her beautiful home. We sat at her table. "Gerda," I said, "It's delicious, but you haven't stopped feeding me since I arrived!" "Jack," she reminded me, "I really didn't eat for three years." Across the table sat her husband Kurt. As a young GI, almost 60 years before, he had found and rescued a 67-pound Gerda Weissmann, then near death. She had lost everything and everybody in her life except for the cherished pictures of her family that she had hidden in the lining of her shoe. She describes it in her book:

I stepped out of the tub. The nurse dried my body and hair. As I stood nude, before a clean, blue and white checkered man's shirt was put on me, I realized abruptly that I possessed nothing, not even a stitch of clothing that I could call my own. I carried only the pictures of Mama, Papa, Arthur, Abek, that I had carried here.

Bags of Letters

In between bites, Gerda told me about the tote bags stacked to the brim with correspondence from kids across the country. There had to have been at least 50 tote bags, each holding several hundred letters. Gerda picked one at random, slit it open and began to read to us. A girl from Minnesota wrote of her anorexia and her deep wish to commit suicide after her father had walked out on her family. But Gerda's story kept her from action. "The Nazis took everything you had. You have NO family left. I realized that at least I could see my father once a month. You are an inspiration! You have given me back my life." This young woman started a suicide hot line in her high school.

And a young woman from Columbine, recent scene of a mass shooting wrote, "I was fat, despairing and felt incompetent. Your book and your presence have given me the strength to speak out about what the Columbine tragedy has meant, and how we all have an obligation never to allow this sort of tragedy to happen again. I was almost too shy to speak up in class. Now I'm giving speeches all over."

Survival is a Privilege and Burden

Looking up from the letter and over her reading glasses, Gerda said, "You see pain must not be wasted." As she says in her book, "Survival is both an exalted privilege and painful burden." This is for me, the most awesome part of Gerda's message—not simply hope, but how she turned her suffering into healing for others.

How people endure, what anchors them, especially in times of terrible suffering, has increasingly claimed my interest, for it's not simply what we do in working with children and youth, but it's why we are doing it and why we choose to go on.

Too soon, our visit ended, and I boarded a plane for Mississippi to deliver a keynote address at a child welfare conference in Hattiesburg. Little did I realize that I carried Gerda's message with me, and its power would manifest itself in a way neither of us could have foreseen.

Cookies and a Ball = Mentors

Those in attendance at the conference were healers—social workers, professionals in mental health and early childhood education, a sprinkling of police, and those who worked in or operated group homes. During the conference, a police officer named Ron Addington, who ran the Juvenile Division for the Picayune, Mississippi, Police Department, talked about how he had gone into some tough public housing areas "with cookies and a ball," luring kids into a game of four square. His efforts eventually grew into a full-fledged sports program, fishing trips, and mentors, especially for kids without fathers.

After my remarks, I was asked to speak to about 40 foster care kids because their speaker had failed to show up. I immediately grabbed Ron, enlisting him to help me with the kids. Given his passionate commitments and what he had said, I knew he would be of great support. I opened up the discussion by asking the kids, "What do you need to succeed?" Hands shot up!

"Love."
"Determination."
"You need to be tough."
"Confidence."
"Education."
"A skill that somebody will pay for."
"An adult that will stick with you."

Their list was uncannily close to the list of resiliency or "protective factors" identified by academics. I told the kids that their list was as good as the researchers'. I asked them whether they had ever seen anyone shot. Almost every hand was raised. Killed? About half the hands. How many of them had seen someone abused physically or sexually. All hands went up. Stunned, I told them this: I live in a pretty nice suburb. There is very little crime. I have not heard of anyone in my town being killed, and, if so, I'm not sure how these suburban kids would have reacted, would have survived. But these kids, they had survived. I spoke about their experience in foster care, how they had something nobody else had, and how they could use their experiences to help others.

Each of the kids had been through rough stuff—school failure, rejection, neglect, physical and sexual abuse, witness to violence. But the gospel of Gerda reached them. I told them, "I know you feel that you are not like other kids, that you are different. That you are wounded, that your experiences have made you weird. But the very fact that you are sitting here, not in jail and not dead, shows how strong you are. You are extraordinary. Most kids would have folded up. You must use your pain to help others."

.

The Hole in Ron's Heart

Then Ron spoke. The kids had moved him to share that he had grown up in foster care, something he had not shared previously. The kids hardly breathed as he told his story. He told the kids about his drunk parents, his abuse, his rebellion, his ponytail, his motorcycle, about being arrested, and of the constant, painful question, "Why me? Why does all this bad stuff happen to me?" About halfway through his story, he told them he was a police officer. Their jaws dropped. He spoke of "the hole in my heart," a "hole that healed when I became a police officer… because I did not want other kids to go through what went through as a youngster… I now know why I had all that pain," he said.

He told the kids that he had been called every bad name in the book—everything they had been called; that he'd been furious with his parents; that no adult had ever stood by him. But he also told the kids of his total commitment to them: "Even if I have to arrest you and put you in handcuffs, I'll call you 'Sir' because you're just someone who's made a mistake. You're not a bad person. Know that. Believe that."

The Gift of Knowing What Kids Need

He concluded, his voice choking, "You have a responsibility to the next generation…that they don't go through what you went through. You don't know how strong you are. And whether you grow up to be police, teachers or parents, you must protect kids and nurture them in ways that you never were. You have the gift of knowing what kids need. You have knowledge and tools that nobody else has."

The room was deathly still. Suddenly, a young, tough-looking, porcelain-hard pretty girl said, "It's happening to my niece, just what happened to me and she's only three years old. I'm going to stand by her. I'm never going to leave her." One wondered: physical abuse? Sexual abuse? She looked over and saw tears streaming down the cheeks of Michael, the head youth worker, their chaperone for the day. And in a wonderfully ingenuous and surprised voice, she said, "Look! Michael's crying." She got up and put her arms around him.

It was an incredibly powerful and deeply moving experience. I had tried to help identify what they would need to make it, but it was Ron who brought it home. They heard from somebody who embodied them, who had every pain they had had, and who had not only made it, but was showing them love and respect for their uniqueness, their potential, and their obligation to others.

But somehow, Gerda Weissmann knew all this…

The welfare of children has always been of utmost importance to me. The abused, the handicapped, the underprivileged, the ill, I can identify with them because I know what it is like not to be able to communicate one's pain and hope. I had learned, above all, that even after cataclysmic events, I was able to laugh again.

Of course I had the resilience of youth on my side. My experiences taught me that all of us have a reservoir of untapped strength that comes to the fore in moments of crisis.

Throughout my years in the camps and against nearly almost insuperable odds, I knew of no one who committed suicide. I wanted to reach out to young people to make them aware of the preciousness of life and show them that it was not to be thrown away thoughtlessly, even under conditions of extreme hardships. I always wanted to impress upon them, how wrong it is to seek a permanent solution to a temporary problem.

(Excerpted from Gerda's book, All But My Life)

None of us goes through life unscathed. Pain can maim. Pain can hobble. But pain can also be used as an instrument of health.

We the wounded healers, helping to heal the unhealed wounders.

ACKNOWLEDGMENTS

For my parents, John Alfred and Helen Fordham, who laid my bedrock values neither by writing them nor preaching them, but by living them;

For my three sisters, Martha, Helen, and Deane, who continue ever so strongly to remind me of these values as they live them;

For my two incredible children, Byron and Hollis, and their spouses Allyss and Tim, respectively, who imbue their growing families with love, joy and concern for others;

For my wonderful wife and lifetime love, Ottilia, who appreciated and understood the heavy demands of my work and who was lovingly supportive with her helpful comments and candid critiques;

For my amazing editor and publisher, Brigette Polmar, Founder of Brand Spoken, for her keen insights, ability to transmute phrases from staid to sparkle, for her patience and inexhaustible humor;

And above all for the many whom I have met over a lifetime, those with whom I have worked from villages in Alaska to the core city in Boston to those running citywide programs of mayors' offices and those laboring on the local, state and federal levels all in their own ways pledged to creating "the beloved community" in which children and their families can thrive. It is they who inspire and continue to inspire. In a very real sense, it is they who have written this book, they who continue to sustain me, to keep my feet moving, to keep on my path.

ABOUT THE AUTHOR

John A. Calhoun

Jack Calhoun has been on his policy walk for more than 50 years working at every level – from tough street corners to an appointment as "Chief Kid for the Country" as President Carter's Commissioner of the U.S. Administration for Children, Youth and Families - to help light the paths to safer communities, stronger families and thriving youth.

As the founder and president of the National Crime Prevention Council, Jack helped to redefine crime prevention from a focus on protection and detention to a mindset of hope: preventing crime, engaging youth and enhancing quality of life by building vital communities that don't produce crime.

An innovator and leader first inspired by the work of Dr. Martin Luther King Jr., Jack has launched several programs that have changed the face – and the policies – of prevention, intervention, support of youth and families, and rehabilitation of offenders. From creating the Office of Domestic Violence Prevention and the Office for Families on the federal level to creating pre-trial diversion programs and victim/victimizer reconciliation initiatives, he has touched the lives and moved the hearts of many along his path. His pioneering work helped to firmly established the faith community as a partner in crime prevention and community building activities through FASTEN, The Faith and Service Technical Education

Network.

As Commissioner of the Department of Youth Services in Massachusetts, he demonstrated to the state – and the nation – that most juvenile offenders could be successfully rehabilitated in a wide variety of highly accountable community-based settings.

Jack ran the McGruff the Crime Dog® "Take a Bite Out of Crime®" campaign for 20 years, building it into one of the most successful public service advertising campaigns in American history.

While serving as the Senior Consultant to the National League of Cities Institute for Youth, Education and Families, Jack founded and directed the California Cities Violence Prevention Network. The groundbreaking initiative brought comprehensive strategies – the blending of prevention, intervention, enforcement and reentry into a single, citywide plan - to a new level. The Network became the template for the U.S. Justice Department's 15-city National Forum on Youth Violence Prevention. Jack currently serves as Senior Consultant to the U.S. Department of Justice for the National Forum.

Jack was a moderator for the Aspen Institute Executive Seminar Program for more than a decade and has lectured at universities across the country, including Harvard, Fordham, Penn, Baylor and more. He continues to be a sought-after moderator and keynote speaker. Jack is the author of two previous books, numerous articles, nationally published editorials, and tool kits designed for his fellow policy walkers.

Married for more than 40 years to his wife Ottilia, Jack is a proud father of two and smitten grandfather of four. He enjoys gardening, travel, tennis, photography, and is a piano player best enjoyed by people with impaired hearing. Jack resides in the National Capital Area.

CAREER TIMELINE

John A. Calhoun

2010 - Present Senior Consultant U.S. Department of Justice and Development Service Group, Inc., for National Forum on Youth Violence Prevention

2006 - 2015 Senior Consultant to National League of Cities Institute for Youth, Education and Families Founder & Director California Cities Violence Prevention Network

2011 Author *Through the Hourglass: Poems of Life and Love*

2004 - 2006 Author *Hope Matters: The Untold Story of How Faith Works in America*

1983 - 2004 President and CEO, National Crime Prevention Council

2001 Doctor of Humane Letters (Honorary), Heidelberg College

1986 Master in Public Administration with Honors, Littauer Fellow, Kennedy School of Government, Harvard University

1981 - 1982 Vice President, Child Welfare League of America

1979 - 1981 Presidential Appointee, Commissioner, U.S. Administration for Children, Youth and Families

1976 - 1979   Gubernatorial Appointee, Commissioner, Massachusetts Department of Youth Services

1973 - 1976   Executive Director, Justice Resource Institute

1970 - 1973   Vice President, Technical Development Corporation

1966 - 1970   Project Officer, Action for Boston Community Development

1965 - 1966   Teacher, Elementary Education, Inner City Philadelphia, PA

1963 - 1965   Master of Divinity, Episcopal Divinity School, Cambridge, MA

1958 - 1963   BA, Brown University

SELECTED AWARDS

John A. Calhoun

2012   Award of Recognition, U.S. Department of Justice, National Forum on Youth Violence Prevention

2011   Leader, Visionary Award from Justice Resource Institute

2004   Lifetime Achievement Award for "Extraordinary Contributions to and Outstanding Service to Youth, Their Families and Communities in America and Throughout the World." Center for Substance Abuse and Prevention, U.S. Department of Health and Human Services

2002   Spirit of Crazy House Award – Reclaiming Youth International Youth Advocate of the Year

1998   Award of Recognition winner, U.S. Office of Juvenile Justice and Delinquency Prevention

1979   Official Citation from the Massachusetts State Senate for "Outstanding and Dedicated Service to Children and Families of the Commonwealth of Massachusetts

1979   Award of recognition from U.S. Attorney General Griffin Bell for Urban Court (Restorative Justice)

1978   Recipient of the American Arbitration Association Award of Recognition

"...I cannot think of a more talented or motivating orator."

-Peggy Conlon
Former President, The Advertising Council, Inc., New York

"I do not know of a more persuasive and effective spokesperson in the nation today for the well-being of children and youth and the communities in which they live than Jack Calhoun."

-Kathy Jett
Former Director, California Dept. of Alcohol and Drug Programs

John A. Calhoun is a frequent keynote speaker, moderator and media guest and is available to speak on the topics covered in *Policy Walking*, as well as those featured on his website HopeMatters.org.

All inquiries can be made via email to hopematters@verizon.net.